Appraisal and Performance Management

About the series

Fast Track is a series of short, practical guides designed to get you up to speed on key business and management skills.

Written by experts with many years' experience in the field, each guide gives you instant access to key tips, advice and guidance – information you can put to work straightaway.

First six titles in the series
Appraisal & Performance Management 1 90429 811 7
Delegation 1 85835 953 8
Leadership 1 85835 963 5
Managing Attendance 1 85835 968 6
Managing Conflict 1 90429 812 5
Managing Time 1 85835 958 9

About the Series Editor
Andrew Forrest is a learning consultant with over 30 years' experience working with and developing people.

Appraisal and Performance Management

Alison Naisby

First published in 2002
Spiro Press
Robert Hyde House
48 Bryanston Square
London W1H 2EA
Telephone: +44 (0)870 400 1000

ISBN 1 90429 811 7

British Library Cataloguing-in-Publication Data.
A catalogue record for this book is available from the
British Library.

**Advice in this book is intended as guidance only. Legislation is subject
to change.**

Printed by: Cromwell Press
Cover image by: Digital Vision
Cover design by: Sign Design

Contents

Introduction

Seismic shifts have taken place in the appraisal process. These include the use of grading systems, performance-related pay, competencies, upwards and 360° appraisal. Experience has shown a clear link between performance management and development, and the results achieved. In order to be most effective, appraisal needs to be part of a wider performance management process.

This book is intended as a guide for managers, supervisors and team leaders; indeed anyone who influences and/or implements the performance appraisal process. If you are such a person, then you face the task of making this process work! This book will help you meet this challenge. The book begins by considering the essential link between performance management and appraisal before offering step-by-step advice on choosing, implementing or enhancing an appraisal system for your organisation. It highlights possible problems and suggests solutions.

Remember, support and advice may also be available from your Human Resources (HR) or Personnel department; both in terms of process and skills.

A useful glossary of terms is included at the end of the book.

Overview of current trends

> This chapter considers:
> > The concept of performance management; trends in appraisal.

Experience has proved that good performance cannot be 'appraised in' at an annual review any more than quality can be 'inspected in' after manufacture. As a result, in many organisations appraisal has developed from being a one-off, annual event into a dynamic, ongoing process of performance management through objectives and staff development.

Some organisations have introduced performance ratings and/or performance-related pay schemes, while others are exploring competencies, upwards and 360° feedback as methods of assessing and enhancing staff development.

Organisations are developing flatter management structures; flexibility, team and project working are becoming increasingly important. In this constantly changing environment, organisations are encouraging individuals to develop a portfolio of skills and take more responsibility for their own performance and development.

The concept of performance management

Performance management establishes the vital link between corporate goals/objectives and the individuals who will implement them. It does this by:

- Breaking corporate goals down into objectives and targets for teams and individuals.
- Managing the process systematically and objectively through regular performance reviews.
- Supporting the performance and development of all staff.

The link between performance and development

The link between performance and development has developed in response to two key questions:

1 How much can you *alter* what has happened in the past?
2 How much can you *influence* what will happen in the future?

Other developments

Competency frameworks

More organisations are developing competency frameworks. Competencies identify the skill/performance factor needed, and then define and describe the standard of competence required. Competencies help to measure skills, abilities and performance factors objectively, enabling appraisals and reviews to be more consistent.

Upwards appraisal

Some organisations make use of upwards appraisals, when managers are appraised by their staff, sometimes through the use of questionnaires. Provided staff are properly briefed about the purpose and objectivity required, upwards appraisals can provide invaluable insight and feedback.

360° appraisal

Organisations with sufficiently open cultures are increasingly using this holistic approach to gather information and feedback from a number of sources. 360° appraisal involves individuals being appraised by all their main contacts. These could include their manager, direct reports, colleagues, customers and suppliers.

This system needs to be well designed and implemented since it is more demanding and time-consuming than other methods of appraisal. However, the benefits can be considerable.

The use of technology

Many organisations have developed and designed their own performance appraisal forms and systems, although some buy in specialised software packages which include forms and systems. Documentation can be sent and completed by e-mail or on the intranet. The sign off and distribution of all relevant copies of documentation can be made simpler, swifter and more secure through the increasing use of technology.

Summary checklist

✓ In recent years appraisal has developed to become part of a more dynamic performance management process.

✓ More companies are developing competencies, upwards and 360° appraisal as effective ways of developing and enhancing staff performance.

✓ More use is being made of technology to speed up and simplify processes.

Performance management and appraisal

This chapter considers and defines:
> Appraisal and the benefits of a performance management system.

A word about terminology

Organisations use different titles and terminology to describe their performance appraisal review process and systems. It is important that the title and objectives are compatible with the aims and culture of the organisation. For example, 'appraisal' or 'annual report' implies an authoritarian, backward-looking approach, while 'performance development review' places the emphasis on encouraging future performance. In this book, the term 'appraisal' has been used throughout as a generic term, incorporating the *performance management* and *appraisal/review* concept.

Performance management

In performance management, the cart cannot come before the horse. Performance must first jointly be managed between the individual and the manager; only then can it be reviewed and appraised.

Performance management involves a partnership between the individual and manager to identify and agree performance objectives, and discuss and implement a joint action plan to meet them. Also to monitor, review and record the individual's performance and results *regularly* in order to guide future actions.

Most performance management approaches share the following elements:

- A sense of purpose, vision and mission, shared and understood by everyone.
- Objectives, which are understandable, measurable and realistic.
- Regular one-to-one discussions to review performance, identify actions and development needs, and set new targets (which the individual can influence).
- Regular team performance reviews to share objectives and targets.
- All staff development is based on skills, performance factors and competencies required for current and probable future job role(s).
- Organisational needs and objectives are known. A training needs analysis is developed for everyone, with timed development plans to meet objectives.

What is appraisal?

The appraisal process involves a yearly or six monthly formal meeting between the individual and manager to review the individual's performance and results. Discussions, objectives, outcomes, future action plans and development needs are recorded on a form. This meeting is supported by shorter, regular review meetings to monitor progress and results ('one-to-ones').

Benefits of a performance management appraisal system

- Creates a link between organisational goals/objectives and the staff responsible for implementing them. Information cascades down.

- Demonstrates commitment by the organisation and managers to staff in terms of interest and time.

- Enhances staff communication/morale (reflected to both internal and external customers, suppliers and potential employees).

- Encourages staff feedback on situations and concerns; provides an opportunity to highlight problems in advance.

- Obtains more objective information on performance results for use in business planning, promotion and remuneration decisions.

- Creates a climate for greater individual and managerial effectiveness, usually reflected in the bottom line.

Summary checklist

Performance management and appraisal involve a partnership between the manager and individual proactively to manage and review job performance throughout the year:

✓ Making the link between corporate goals and those who will carry them out.

✓ Managing the process objectively by setting clear objectives, standards and targets.

✓ Holding regular one-to-one reviews and appraisals to monitor progress.

✓ Supporting future staff performance and development through timed action plans to develop and train individuals.

The company ethos

This chapter considers:
> The importance of the organisation's vision; its clarity of purpose.
> How the organisation's mission/objectives are cascaded down and apportioned at every level.

The company ethos

In the most successful organisations the appraisal process is driven from the top down. Directors and senior managers have developed the organisation's vision, mission and possibly values statements, which are shared with everyone. Without a clear understanding of what these are, your appraisal system will fail to achieve your organisation's goals.

Vision

The vision is the organisation's aim, which gives a clear sense of direction.

Mission

The mission is set out in a mission statement:

- What the organisation is in business to achieve.
- How it will do this.
- Where it sees itself in the future.

Values

Values statements show the *beliefs* the organisation holds, which *guide daily staff decisions/actions.*

Shared with people at all levels, the vision, mission and values answer the vital question *why?*, which supplies the motivation. The diagram overleaf illustrates this concept.

What do you do if there is no vision?

In some newer or smaller companies, vision, mission and values statements have not yet been developed or updated and shared with everyone.

Question
"What if we don't have a mission statement or clear objectives? It's as if we haven't got a compass. We don't know where we're going, let alone how to get there."

Possible solutions
- Raise the subject with an appropriate manager and/or the HR department. Meanwhile, don't sit back and wait.

- Develop your own mission statement for your team, based on team objectives.

- Hold a team meeting, explain about objectives, get input.

- Get agreement with 'ownership' of the objectives.

The performance management cascade

VISION, MISSION
VALUES STATEMENTS
PURPOSE

COMPANY GOALS
STRATEGIC OBJECTIVES
BUSINESS PLAN

DIVISIONAL OR DEPARTMENTAL
GOALS, OBJECTIVES

KEY RESULT AREAS, MEASUREMENTS

UNIT, BRANCH OR TEAM
GOALS, OBJECTIVES

KEY RESULT AREAS, MEASUREMENTS, TARGETS

INDIVIDUALS' OBJECTIVES
KEY RESULT AREAS, STANDARDS, COMPETENCIES, TARGETS
PERSONAL DEVELOPMENT OBJECTIVES, PLANS
(ALIGNED TO TEAM/COMPANY OBJECTIVES)

REGULAR EVALUATION, REVIEWS, PERFORMANCE APPRAISAL

From the vision, mission and values:

- Organisational goals and objectives are devolved and delegated down through divisions, departments and teams to individuals.

- Performance is then aligned with, and contributes towards meeting, organisational objectives through individuals' key result areas.

- The process is underpinned by reviews and performance appraisal for *everyone*, based on a commitment to a minimum organisational policy (see chapter 4).

- Consult the team; identify the key result areas – what needs to be done, by whom and by when.
- By getting team 'buy in' you can start to improve team performance to meet objectives, and influence others.

As a manager, supervisor or team leader, it is your responsibility to find a method of sharing the organisation's goals with staff in a clear, enthusiastic and motivational way. You need to make sure that:

- Staff understand their individual job and team objectives (what they are there to achieve).
- The key result areas (key tasks and responsibilities) enable your staff to meet their objectives.
- Staff understand their contribution to organisational goals.

Your organisation's culture and ethos should inform your choice of appraisal scheme.

Summary checklist

✓ Find out how your organisation's mission, objectives and business plan cascade down to departments and teams. If they are not evident or available, ask for them.

✓ If some of the above are not yet implemented, meet with your team to agree their objectives, key tasks, individual actions and deadlines. Consider how they contribute to meeting organisational objectives.

Building a performance appraisal system

This chapter describes:
> The 'House of Appraisal' – a model for all appraisal systems:

- Firm foundation – company ethos.
  - minimum organisational policy.
  - performance appraisal system.
- Ground floor – job descriptions, objectives.
  - key result areas.
  - standards, competencies and targets.
- First floor – preparation and planning.
- Second floor – performance appraisal and action plans.
- Roof – personal development plans.
  - implementation, one-to-one reviews.

Building a performance appraisal system is similar to building a house, with a number of key stages. Whether the appraisal is held annually or six monthly, it needs to be the *culmination* of a continuous, planned performance management process.

The house of appraisal

The diagram overleaf provides a template for the key stages in building a successful appraisal system. Organisations may develop systems along various lines; however, to be successful, these key elements need to be present, and recognisable.

Key stages

Firm foundation – laid by directors and senior managers

A firm foundation consists of three parts:

1 The organisational or company ethos
Linked to their values system (see previous chapter).

2 A minimum organisational performance appraisal policy
Underpinning the ethos (see p. 15).

3 An appraisal and review system
Based on a logical, *dependency sequence* (when one action is dependent on another being carried out first; see chapter 16). Appropriate supporting documentation.

The house of appraisal

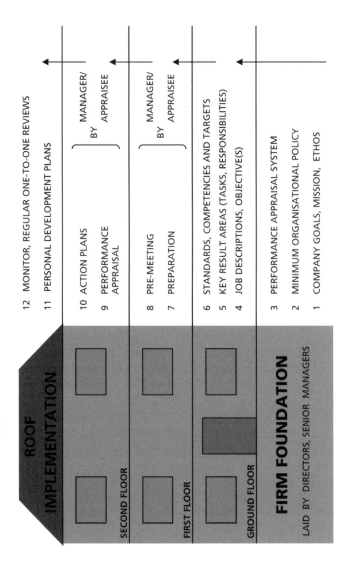

ROOF
IMPLEMENTATION

SECOND FLOOR

FIRST FLOOR

GROUND FLOOR

FIRM FOUNDATION

LAID BY DIRECTORS, SENIOR MANAGERS

12 MONITOR, REGULAR ONE-TO-ONE REVIEWS
11 PERSONAL DEVELOPMENT PLANS

10 ACTION PLANS
9   PERFORMANCE APPRAISAL
BY MANAGER/APPRAISEE

8   PRE-MEETING
7   PREPARATION
BY MANAGER/APPRAISEE

6   STANDARDS, COMPETENCIES AND TARGETS
5   KEY RESULT AREAS (TASKS, RESPONSIBILITIES)
4   JOB DESCRIPTIONS, OBJECTIVE(S)

3   PERFORMANCE APPRAISAL SYSTEM
2   MINIMUM ORGANISATIONAL POLICY
1   COMPANY GOALS, MISSION, ETHOS

Performance appraisal – a minimum organisational policy

The most successful schemes depend on organisations developing the following commitments:

- Senior management are committed, involved and appraised themselves.

- Personal objectives and targets are aligned with organisational and departmental objectives.

- Appraisals and reviews are part of a continuous performance management process.

- The objectives, and how the scheme operates, are explained to everyone.

- All line managers receive training in performance appraisal, and the skills required.

- Methods of reviewing performance are objective and regular; the system is monitored by a senior individual responsible for consistency and results.

- The immediate manager conducts the appraisal, at least once a year.

- Both parties prepare in writing.

- The main focus should be on future performance, development, targets and action plans.

- Individuals have a personal development plan which records training and development needs, implementation and timescales.

Ground floor

The ground floor provides the way in through:

4 Job descriptions

Drawn up through consultation, relevant and specific, showing:

- Objectives.
- Accountability.
- Key tasks and responsibilities.

5 Key result areas

The tasks and responsibilities which *must* be carried out to meet the job objectives.

6 Standards, competencies and targets

Minimum standards of performance for tasks and responsibilities. The manager should also set specific measurable targets for individuals to improve and develop performance.

First floor

7 Preparation

This consists of all the prior planning and preparation by the manager and individual, to enable the appraisal to take place effectively.

8 Pre-meeting

A pre-meeting briefing is particularly important when the system has changed or the manager has not appraised the individual before (see pre-meeting agenda chapter 16).

The time and effort invested will largely determine the appraisal outcome; 'Fail to prepare and you prepare to fail'.

Second floor

9 The performance appraisal
Consists of three parts:

- A review of the past, from which to learn.
- A preview of the future, to set objectives, standards and targets, and to improve performance.
- The identification of training and development needs.

10 Action plans
To identify:

- Specific actions required, accountability and deadlines.
- Support and training needed to aid the individual's improvement and development.

This process is usually monitored by the manager's manager, who reviews and signs the appraisal.

Roof – implementation

As a manager, you need to ensure that the appraisal is part of a continuous performance management process through:

11 Personal development plans
To record the route and timescale by which individuals will be supported and trained (see chapter 16 for an example).

12 Regular one-to-one reviews
To monitor and evaluate performance and progress against objectives, key result areas, standards, targets and projects.

As one-to-one reviews are such an important part of the appraisal process they are discussed in more detail overleaf.

One-to-one reviews

Regular one-to-ones reviews are essential to the success of the appraisal process. One-to-ones are structured and recorded review meetings which allow both managers and staff to evaluate performance and results, regularly. An ideal structure is shown on the review form opposite. This structure ensures a positive start, covering achievements, improvements and constraints. It encourages sharing feedback and concludes with focused action planning by *both* parties.

Frequency

As an absolute minimum, staff should never have less than three reviews and one appraisal per year. Many managers hold them monthly or bi-monthly. In constantly changing environments, managers should hold short reviews more frequently to update objectives, review and set targets, and maintain focus.

Length

Reviews will vary from around twenty minutes to one and a half hours, depending on their frequency, content and the seniority of staff involved.

Preparation

Staff need the review form and guidance notes in good time to allow adequate preparation for the one-to-one. They need to consider their performance and feedback and write brief notes, giving examples. Managers need to do the same. This saves time at one-to-ones, and ensures both parties are focused.

One-to-one review form

NAME _____ MANAGER _____

DATE _____ Continue overleaf if necessary

REVIEW OF PERFORMANCE SINCE LAST MEETING

ACHIEVEMENTS – in objectives, key tasks, targets, etc

CONCERNS, AREAS FOR IMPROVEMENT

CHANGES, CONSTRAINTS

FEEDBACK – FROM COLLEAGUES, CUSTOMERS
(Praise, thanks, recommendations, complaints)

AGREED ACTION/AREAS TO WORK ON BY
Reviewee:

Manager:

Signatures: Reviewee   Manager

Conducting reviews

First managers must ask the individual to review the last period, following the headings outlined in the one-to-one review form. Managers should then ask 'open' questions (requiring more than a straight 'yes' or 'no' answer) to probe and check facts and assumptions, opening up a dialogue to share ideas and feedback, and address issues.

From this discussion the 'agreed review' (often written in the form of bullet points) is finalised and signed by both parties. Any strong disagreement should be noted. Both parties should keep copies of the agreed review for reference at subsequent appraisals.

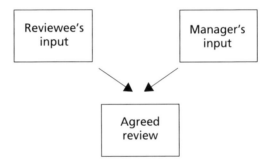

Benefits of regular one-to-one reviews

- Provides a structured *overview* of performance during the period.

- Provides regular two-way communication and feedback.

- Allows the manager to have their 'finger on the pulse' – reviewing, re-focusing objectives, targets, job descriptions, etc.

- Underpins the appraisal process.

- Records the year's performance, saves time, helps accurate preparation to review the whole year.

- Provides a rehearsal for managers and staff new to one other, or the process.

Updating records

Objectives, targets, job descriptions and training plans need to be updated after one-to-one reviews, and new standards and targets set, where appropriate.

Summary checklist

✓ The 'House of Appraisal' model shows the key stages for building a successful appraisal system.

✓ Such a system needs to be based on a minimum organisational policy, implemented in stages, following the dependency sequence.

✓ It needs to be underpinned by regular, recorded one-to-one reviews to monitor progress, maintain focus and aid appraisal preparation.

5

Introducing or updating a performance appraisal scheme

This chapter covers:
> Deciding on the type of appraisal scheme – the implications.
> The importance of management and staff involvement.

Management and staff involvement

When introducing or updating an appraisal scheme, it is important to get 'buy in' in from the users by:

- Explaining *why* performance appraisal is being introduced or revised.
- Involving managers in the evolution of the scheme.
- Trialing a draft scheme with representative departments.
- Using feedback and ideas to improve the scheme, to help sell the idea to the rest of the organisation.

Deciding on the type of scheme – the implications

When considering the type of scheme and its operation, there are many issues to consider. Key introductory or updating steps are:

1 Decide your objectives; how the scheme will help achieve organisational goals.

2 Ensure commitment at a senior level.

3 Decide who is involved and who will have overall responsibility.

4 Decide the most suitable type of scheme, or aspects of a scheme:

   4.1 Traditional appraisal?

   4.2 Competency-based appraisal?

   4.3 Performance-related pay?

   4.4 Upwards or 360° appraisal?

   4.5 The title – what's in a name?

5 Consider the structure of the scheme:

   5.1 Frequency and timing?

   5.2 Paperwork and guidance notes?

   5.3 What supporting information will be produced?

   5.4 How will any information acquired be monitored and used – eg to influence training, development, promotion, salary, succession planning?

6 Produce the required documentation.

7 Communicate the objectives and methods of the scheme to everyone.

8 Decide how and when to train the appraisers.

9 Monitor the early stages closely and review results within a deadline.

10 Be flexible; make necessary adjustments.

Factors to consider further

1 Organisational objectives

Organisations have different agendas for their schemes. It is vital that the organisation makes it clear *why* it is implementing or re-designing a scheme so managers can inform their staff. Appraisal is normally about the alignment of objectives, fine-tuning and developing an individual's future performance to contribute to meeting organisational objectives.

2 Ensure commitment at a senior level

In order for any appraisal system to succeed it must be driven from the top down. This requires full support, involvement and implementation by directors and senior managers.

3 Involvement and responsibility

This is based on the commitment made by directors and senior managers in their minimum organisational appraisal policy.

Performance appraisal – best practice

These guidelines apply to all types of appraisal. (Remember, though, that with 360° appraisal the individual is appraised by all their main contacts, who might produce individual action plans.)

- All staff need to have a discussion *at least once a year* with their manager about their performance. The discussion should recognise achievements and good performance, and address any areas of weakness. Most of the content should relate to the future and result in an action plan for the individual which includes specific targets. Training and development needs should be identified.

- The manager also needs to complete an action plan, showing what he/she intends to do to support, coach, develop and train the individual.

- The training and development needs, means of implementing them and appropriate timescales should be recorded on a personal development plan, given to the individual.

- The principal line manager is responsible for seeing that this is done.

- Both managers and staff should prepare for the appraisal in writing, and have input on previous performance, future priorities, actions and targets.

- The jobholder should be encouraged to self-appraise, and their views taken into account.

- Either then, or soon after, performance standards against key result areas should be agreed, and a limited number of important targets set.

- Throughout the year, performance against these key result areas, standards and targets should be monitored regularly at one-to-one review meetings.

These guidelines are distilled wisdom from the experience of many organisational schemes. They are applicable to any type or size of organisation, who can benchmark their procedures against them.

4 Decide the type of scheme

Below is a brief outline of different types of schemes. The following chapter looks at them in more detail.

4.1 Traditional appraisal

Traditional appraisal involves the manager appraising the performance of their staff.

People are likely to work more effectively if they are provided with relevant, meaningful and accurate information about their levels of performance, abilities and competencies. Depending on the organisational culture/style and the attitude and skill of the manager, these conversations can vary from, at best, a well prepared, two-way discussion to, at worst, an authoritarian 'tell session'.

4.2 Competency-based appraisal

Competencies are behavioural skills which can be observed, evaluated and modified by developmental activities. They are *not* about personality or character traits. Competencies are clearly identified and defined. Performance is appraised against them.

4.3 Performance-related pay schemes

• Involve some method of relating performance to pay.

• Schemes vary widely in different organisations; rewards can encompass bonuses, commission and piece rates, as well as profit sharing or some other form of performance-related pay.

• Organisations need to devise objective and fair systems to measure performance, and relate it to financial reward (see chapter 9 for more information).

4.4 Upwards or 360° degree appraisal

In upwards or 360° appraisal, managers are appraised by their staff or teams and internal 'customers'. These systems are either based on face-to-face questions and feedback or the use of a questionnaire, which can be attributed or completed confidentially.

Upwards appraisal
Here the focus is on the *manager* seeking information and feedback from staff to improve their managerial skills and performance.

Irrespective of whether your scheme incorporates upwards appraisal, as a manager you should implement a *two-way process*. You need to explain that you will be asking for feedback on your skills, abilities, attitudes and behaviour as a manager, and what you can do to further improve.

360° appraisal

Some organisations use 360° appraisal, which involves all-round feedback – from colleagues, internal and sometimes external 'customers'.

For more information about conducting successful upwards or 360° appraisals see chapter 14.

4.5 The title – what's in a name?

Choosing the right title for your appraisal system is best left until all the components of the scheme have been finalised. Often the name encapsulates the organisation's ethos and objectives, for example, 'appraisal' or 'annual report' implies an authoritarian, backward-looking appraisal, a 'telling' session by the manager. On the other hand, 'performance management and development review' implies a more open, forward-looking, no-blame culture. Some mistakes are expected, but they are used as learning opportunities. Emphasis is put on:

- A consultative approach to encourage self-appraisal of performance.

- Mutual developmental feedback.
- Coaching, mentoring, planning and supporting future performance to maintain continuous improvement.

Another option is 'performance review and planning agreement.' This encapsulates the concept of a compact between the manager and staff, with the emphasis on planning the agreement for the year ahead.

5 Consider the structure of the scheme

5.1 Frequency and timing
Some appraisals are conducted six monthly, others annually. Whatever their frequency, it is important that they are underpinned by regular one-to-one review meetings. For timings, organisations use one of two methods:

1 Seasonal
All appraisals are co-ordinated and carried out at the same time, six monthly or annually, sometimes linked to year-end.

What if you don't have enough time?

Question
"I have got 14 staff to appraise but we are only given the month of March to complete them. How can I invest the time needed, manage the team and do my job as well?"

Possible solutions
- Discuss the situation with your manager.
- Explain the amount of time required to make the appraisals meaningful.
- Explore the need/possibility of appointing a team leader who could appraise part of the team.

- Negotiate an extended period of six weeks to two months to balance your workload and complete meaningful appraisals.

2 A rolling timetable

This is usually based on the anniversary date an individual joined the organisation, or their last promotion date.

The main benefits of this approach are:

- It is less disruptive; managers can integrate other responsibilities and appraisals into their workload. (Ideally managers should not appraise more than 15 direct reports because of the amount of time required to manage staff performance.)

- It prevents going through the appraisal process with individuals who are too new in post to be evaluated fairly.

5.2 Paperwork and guidance notes

Managers will need to familiarise themselves with the paperwork and systems in order to brief staff clearly.

The remaining key steps – 5.3, 5.4 and items 6–7 and 9–10 – are not covered here since they are mainly the responsibility of the HR department. However, number 8, training the appraisers, does concern managers so some advice is offered below.

What if you feel out of your depth?

Question

"I have recently been promoted and now manage a team of four. Although I've *been* appraised a couple of times, I am now expected to appraise my new team without any real training. I have never managed staff before and feel out of my depth."

Possible solutions

Conducting a competent and motivational appraisal is a complex process. It requires both knowledge and skills that have to be acquired, learnt and *practised*. It is therefore important for managers to ask for, and make sure they receive, training and support. You could usefully read up about the subject or watch a video/CD-ROM. Alternatively, you could attend a training course or, if possible, observe a more experienced manager appraising.

Summary checklist

✓ Ensure top-level commitment to introducing, updating, trialing or implementing an appraisal scheme.

✓ Ensure manager and staff involvement, and training.

✓ Identify and communicate the organisation's objectives.

✓ Ensure understanding and 'buy in' to the appraisal system.

✓ Design the logistics; consider deadlines to avoid time pressures.

✓ Benchmark your organisation's appraisal system against best practice.

6

Selecting an appraisal scheme

This chapter identifies:
> The main benefits and drawbacks of different types of appraisal schemes.
> What to consider in selecting a scheme that is best suited to your organisational needs.

Appraisal schemes

Traditional appraisal

Benefits

- Performance overview – at least annually the manager and individual appraisee prepare for, and jointly review, performance in a two-way, structured discussion with feedback to review and record progress and action planning.

- One-to-one reviews – regular, structured review meetings take place to monitor progress.

- Records – both parties keep records of these review meetings as evidence for future reference, or for disciplinary procedures.

- Action planning – both parties write action plans identifying their input, to improve future performance.

- Development and training needs – these are identified and incorporated into a training and development plan, with actions, accountability and deadlines for implementation.
- Simplicity – the simplest, least time-consuming appraisal to design and implement.

Drawbacks
Feedback tends to be one way, unless the manager has the inclination, confidence and skills actively to seek feedback on his/her performance.

Competency-based appraisal

Benefits
- Identification – the performance factors, skills and input required for the job are clearly identified.
- Definitions and consistency – all managers and staff work to the same competency definitions to define the input required. This provides consistency across the organisation.
- Language – competency definitions provide a measure and language to identify examples and evidence to discuss performance. Competency definitions should be structured as short phrases, using plenty of active verbs.
- Gains specific self-assessment – the manager first asks the individual to assess their own level of competence. This avoids damaging working relationships when performance is unsatisfactory as individuals may be able to identify their own under-performance, rather than having the manager *tell* them. This approach helps managers who find it difficult to discuss under-performance, and may consequently avoid the issue.

- Objectivity – because discussion is based on identified competencies and facts, backed up by valid evidence and behavioural examples, it is *objective* rather than subjective.
- Action planning and training – action planning and training is based on specifically identified needs to achieve the required performance against competencies.

Drawbacks

- A high level of management and staff input is required in terms of knowledge, skill and time to research, develop and agree relevant competencies.
- This requires excellent co-ordination and communication between HR and managers.
- All staff need to be inducted, and managers trained, in the understanding and implementation of competencies.

Performance-related pay schemes

Benefits

- Financial recognition – enables companies to recognise excellent achievements and results and to reward them through financial incentives. This involves identifying the type of contribution to be rewarded, and the criteria.
- Differentials – the system illustrates equality for similar jobs and shows differentials for different jobs and motivational levels.
- Incentive – money can be a motivator to give a high level of commitment. However, most staff also require a challenge, job satisfaction and an opportunity for self-development and promotion.
- Calibre of staff – money can be a way of attracting and retaining top calibre staff, particularly when demand outstrips supply.

Drawbacks

- Designing the optimum scheme is time-consuming and complex.
- It must be fair, and measurable.
- Performance-related pay *can* act as a de-motivator if it is linked to inappropriate or unachievable targets.
- The appraisal and salary review should be *two separate processes*, handled at *different times.* If they are not adequately de-linked, the focus will be on *reward* rather than performance.

Upwards appraisal

Benefits

- A two-way process – upwards appraisal is a process of giving and receiving information and feedback by *both* parties. Organisations have introduced it to help managers who may not have the inclination, skills or confidence to ask for feedback, to help them manage more effectively.
- Insight and awareness – increasingly, organisations realise that the person best able to comment on a manager's effectiveness and processes is the individual being managed. This gives managers greater insight into their personal 'strengths and weaknesses' and reveals how their actions and behaviour are perceived, and the impact this has on their direct reports.
- Identifies strengths and weaknesses – consistent messages from several sources will confirm strengths, positive behaviours and results. They also make it difficult for managers to deny or ignore any 'weaknesses', negative actions or behaviour – and their consequences.
- Creates a positive, customer-focused culture – the growing importance of customer service has created awareness of the concept of the 'internal customer'. Organisations and managers

now realise that they have internal customers who need to be invited to comment, and their feedback listened to. This helps to develop an open, informed, no-blame culture, where seeking feedback to create awareness and improve performance 'is part of the way we operate'. Individuals also feel more consulted and therefore empowered.

Drawbacks

- The organisational ethos may not be supportive to feedback and upwards appraisal.

- Upwards appraisal is more time-consuming and complex to organise and implement.

- Unless it is well planned, and all individuals briefed and trained on the objectives, process and implementation, it can be threatening to the manager or provide an opportunity for staff to 'settle scores'. Some organisations collate the information and feed it back via a third party, skilled at interpreting data and giving feedback. This may be an external consultant, involving additional costs. However, this approach does ensure anonymity for appraisers.

360° appraisal

Benefits

- An holistic approach – 360° appraisal provides all-round feedback – from staff, colleagues, internal and sometimes external customers or suppliers. People can then evaluate their impact on these individuals and use this knowledge to improve results and relationships.

- Cultural change – in this fast-changing, competitive world, organisations need empowered people who can use their initiative to provide rapid, flexible responses. To change from managing to *leading*.

- Achieves business objectives – through holistic feedback, greater self-awareness and continuous improvement which releases people's full energies and talents.

Drawbacks

- Although the process has the potential to deliver many benefits, it is not suitable for every organisation because of its complexity.
- 360° appraisal requires the most research, preparation time, knowledge to develop and skills to implement.
- It requires reciprocal openness, honesty and respect – it would be inappropriate in a complacent, top-down or blame culture, where little or no feedback is given.
- 360° appraisal will raise expectations and identify training and development needs. As a result, it would be counterproductive to introduce it if inadequate support and follow-up systems are in place.

Factors to consider in selecting the scheme

Selecting the optimum scheme for an organisation is a complex judgement. The primary factors to consider are the organisation's *ethos and culture*:

1 Is the organisation run on more traditional, authoritarian 'command and control' lines?

Traditional 'command and control'

2   Or is it a more customer-focused organisation, where the main management role is seen in terms of improving processes to support and empower colleagues? They in turn support and provide service excellence to *external* customers.

Customer-focused 'support and empower'

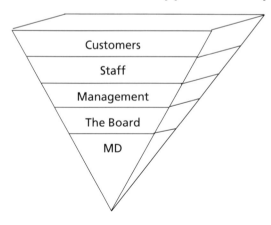

One way of identifying whether your organisation's culture is traditional or customer-focused is to consider the skills that are practised and valued there.

Traditional	Customer-focused
1 Scheduling and planning.	1 Agreeing objectives and task parameters.
2 Supervising and organising subordinates.	2 Consulting staff to achieve 'buy in'.
3 Directing – giving instructions.	3 Briefing clearly, getting agreement.
4 Progress chasing and monitoring.	4 Communication – asking, listening, acknowledging, clarifying.
5 Setting targets and deadlines.	5 Agreeing measurable standards and targets.
6 Checking for and rectifying non-conformance.	6 Providing developmental opportunities.
7 On-the-job training.	7 Coaching, leading by example, motivating.
8 Giving criticism.	8 Providing feedback.
9 Monitoring tasks regularly.	9 Monitoring and reviewing progress regularly.
10 Motivating (through reward and punishment).	10 Encouraging self-empowerment.

Once the organisation's culture has been identified, it is easier to reach decisions about which appraisal scheme, or combination of scheme(s), would be most appropriate. Consider the current position in your organisation.

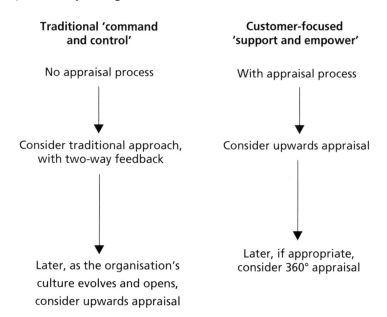

Traditional 'command and control'

No appraisal process

Consider traditional approach, with two-way feedback

Later, as the organisation's culture evolves and opens, consider upwards appraisal

Customer-focused 'support and empower'

With appraisal process

Consider upwards appraisal

Later, if appropriate, consider 360° appraisal

Summary checklist

✓ Consider the benefits and drawbacks of each type, or combination, of appraisal scheme(s).

✓ Also take into account the organisation's ethos, culture and typical skills to decide the optimum scheme.

✓ Get each system established before considering a logical progression.

Achieving the best from people

This chapter covers:
> The six key questions people must have answers to in order to 'buy in' to the appraisal process.
> Job descriptions and summaries; their content and how to draw them up.

"If you don't know where you are going, any road will get you there". Peter Drucker, management guru

Achieving the best from people

To get the very best from people and ensure their commitment to the appraisal process, people *must know* the answers to six key questions (see flowchart overleaf).

Six key questions

1 What is the broader picture?

The performance management cascade on p. 10 demonstrates the importance of people understanding the organisation's vision,

Achieving the best from people

In order to commit to the appraisal process people must know:

1 What is the broader picture?
– Vision, mission, values statements
– Company goals, objectives

2 What is my job?
– Job description/summary
– Clear accountability, reporting structure
– Key responsibilities and relationships

a) What are my objectives?
– Job objectives, individual objectives (aligned to department and company objectives)

b) What are my key result areas?
– Key tasks, responsibilities – to achieve objectives (aligned to department, project and team objectives)

3 To what standards?
– Standards and competencies for the job
– 'SMART' – measurable six ways
– So I can self-appraise

4 How am I doing?
– Monitoring, regular one-to-one reviews
– Preparation for performance appraisal
– Performance appraisal, feedback

5 Where am I going?
– Action planning

c) Short-term targets
– Motivators, show way ahead, how and when to get there

d) Medium/long-term targets
– Career development. Future potential

6 How do I get there?
– Development objectives, personal development plans
– Regular one-to-ones to review performance, progress
– Support, training, coaching, mentoring, special projects

mission and values. These answer the question *why? – why should I do this?* People need to understand the value of their job, and how it contributes to meeting organisational, business and team objectives.

2 What is my job?

This flags up the importance of the job description/summary which provides up-to-date information on *why* the job exists, *what* is the nature of the job, and the outcomes required.

a) What are my objectives?

Individuals need to have a clear, up-to-date understanding of what they are employed to do. Individual and job objectives should answer three key questions:

- **Why the job matters** – the contribution it makes.
- **What someone is being employed for** – key tasks, responsibilities, outcomes.
- **How they can achieve these outcomes** – the input, means and methods.

b) What are my key result areas?

Key tasks and responsibilities an individual must carry out in order to focus on, and meet, their job objectives.

3 To what standards?

Standards of performance and competencies for the job.

4 How am I doing?

Individuals need regularly to self-appraise performance against standards and competencies. One-to-one reviews and appraisals provide a more detailed, structured overview.

5 Where am I going?

c) Short-term targets
Measurable, specific, timed targets, set through consultation.

d) Medium/long-term targets
Assessment of the individual's future potential, training and development needs and career development strategy.

6 How do I get there?

Through:

- Clear, specific development objectives.
- Regular one-to-ones and appraisals to review and monitor progress.
- Ongoing support, coaching and training, listed on a personal development plan.

Job descriptions

Since job descriptions are an *essential element* of achieving the best from people, it is useful to consider their contents, and how they are drawn up or revised.

What goes on a job description?

The content and order of job descriptions vary considerably between organisations. However, the *job title* (and possibly location) are usually followed by *accountability* (showing how the job fits in to the department or organisation), *job dimensions* and *key working relationships*. Then follow the *objective(s), main tasks, responsibilities* and *required outcomes*.

Job description content

Job title – which reflects the job content (does not imply the sex of the holder)

Location – where the job is based or carried out

Accountability, reporting structure (if appropriate, an organisational chart) – showing how the job fits in to the department or organisation and to whom the jobholder is accountable

Job dimensions, responsibilities – major responsibilities, eg for staff, equipment, materials, consumables, budgets, plant, machinery, legal requirements etc

Key working relationships – internally and externally

Objectives – an overall statement of the purpose of the job and role, linked to outcomes (may include personal job objectives)

Key result areas (linked to outcomes) – a thorough analysis of the tasks/duties, responsibilities and outcomes to achieve objectives

Performance standards (may be listed separately) – an outline of acceptable standards of performance and/or competencies to achieve the required objectives and outcomes

Working conditions – relevant to the job; travelling, working unsociable hours or from home, etc

Training and development – available to help the jobholder's performance

The manager's responsibilities

A particular management skill is the ability to align the job objectives and key result areas with the team and company objectives, and to apportion them fairly among staff.

Job summaries

In some fast-moving organisations change is a constant; flexibility and team working are essential. Such organisations often find job summaries more suitable than job descriptions as they are less prescriptive, simpler, more concise and provide greater flexibility within job roles.

Job summary content

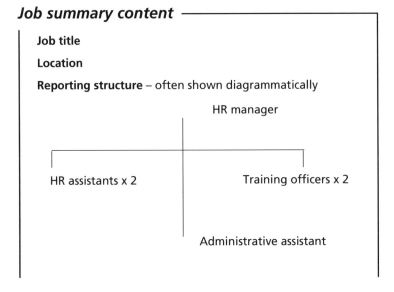

Job title

Location

Reporting structure – often shown diagrammatically

HR manager

HR assistants x 2   Training officers x 2

Administrative assistant

> **Job objectives**
>
> **Responsibilities**
>
> **Relationships**
>
> **Key result areas/tasks** – numbered and listed
>
> **Performance standards** – numbered and listed

Some organisations list performance standards on the summary, others list them separately (see chapter 8).

Why, what and how format

Both the job description/summary content follows the *why, what* and *how* format. The *why* is the essential factor that *motivates* and provides the *reason* for the 'what and how'.

For example, a supervisor who shouts "Get down to goods-in immediately" would get more willing commitment if they added "because the urgent delivery has arrived." *Why* is the motivator.

Or even try the motivator first. "The urgent missing delivery has arrived, you are needed in goods-in immediately, thanks." If people understand *why* they are much more likely to be motivated to co-operate.

Job descriptions should be well-used reference documents

Managers need to ensure that all their staff have relevant, up-to-date job descriptions, revised regularly.

For both parties the benefits are:

- Knowing exactly what the job consists of.
- Knowing where effort needs to be focused to fulfil job objectives and improve performance.

- Working *smarter* not harder.
- Achieving greater self-development and job satisfaction.

What if there are no job descriptions or summaries?

Question

"Our new HR manager wants all staff job descriptions written or updated before this year's appraisals start. Some of my staff don't even have job descriptions, those we have are out of date, even irrelevant. How do I go about drawing them up? As the content has changed, how on earth do I get staff to agree them? They'll probably think I'm trying to get more work out of them."

Possible solution

A good way to handle this situation is to explain that you (the manager/job holder(s)) are going to *consult* and draw up/update the job descriptions. Use inclusive language – 'we', 'us', 'our', 'together' or 'jointly'.

How to write/revise job descriptions to achieve 'buy in'

Job descriptions are written on the *job* not the individual, so staff who have 'unique' jobs need to prepare individually, while those with identical jobs can work together.

- Individually, or as a team, brief your staff on the reason for the new or updated job description. Explain that you are consulting them for their ideas and input, since *they* are doing the job(s).

Change, doing something new, different or extra often provokes resistance. People always ask "What's in it for me?", so *sell the benefits for them*.

- Give your staff the list of headings from your job descriptions (if available) or use those from our suggested document (see p. 45).

- Clarify what the headings mean and what needs be included in each section.

There are two methods to achieve 'buy in':

1 Individually
Both the individual and manager use these headings to write their versions of the job description.

2 As a group
Staff with identical jobs can either work alone or brainstorm together. It can be helpful for the manager to record the suggestions on a flipchart. Manager and staff then compare notes, discuss areas of divergence and agree through consultation what the job actually consists of.

Where divergence occurs it may be because the nature of the job has changed, and one party may not be aware of this, or the individual may be taking on additional tasks, or neglecting others, because of outside pressures or personal preferences.

Difficulties with job descriptions often arise because of non-existent, unclear or changing objectives or because key result areas and responsibilities are unclearly defined, or unaligned to meet objectives. Therefore staff are *not* focusing on the key areas and responsibilities that will achieve the objectives.

The job description/summary is then finalised and dated. Copies need to go to:

- The jobholder.
- The manager.

- The HR department.

A short one-to-one meeting can then be held with the jobholder to motivate and focus the individual, and link the job description with their objectives, key tasks and responsibilities.

Summary checklist

✓ Achieve people's commitment to the appraisal process by answering six key questions:

1 What is the broader picture? – vision, mission, objectives.

2 What is my job? – job description/summary; job objectives; key result areas.

3 To what standards/competencies?

4 How am I doing? – through regular one-to-one reviews and appraisals.

5 Where am I going? – future targets and development.

6 How do I get there? – regular reviews; personal development plans; ongoing support, training, coaching and mentoring.

✓ Ensure you draw up effective job descriptions and summaries (through consultation).

Measuring performance – key result areas, standards and targets

> This chapter offers advice on:
> > Making the best use of appraisal forms.
> > Using ratings, discussing performance, gaining self-assessment.
> > Setting and measuring objectives, key result areas, standards and targets.

Whether there is a requirement for measuring performance connects back to the different agendas organisations have for their appraisal schemes.

A flexible and open approach

Some appraisals are based on a 'blank piece of paper' approach, reviewing from headings the objectives and outcomes. The dialogue mainly dictates the focus of the appraisal. This requires a high level of training and skill on the manager's part to lead discussions objectively.

This approach does not work well when the organisation requires some type of rating because of major implications relating to objectivity and consistency.

Appraisal forms

Many organisations use forms to structure the discussion. These forms need careful consideration at the design stage, particularly if a rating system is also being used which may involve an element of performance-related pay.

Example

PERFORMANCE FACTORS	Comment on specific strengths/ weaknesses, achievements, etc
QUALITY OF WORK Consistent high quality in all aspects ☐ Good in most aspects ☐ Of varying quality ☐ Unacceptable ☐	

Forms – categories and combinations

- Open forms with headings.
- Statements with numbers or tick boxes, limited room to comment.
- Competencies and/or service-level agreements.
- Combinations of the above formats.
- Upwards or 360° appraisals, with questionnaires.

Appraisal forms – best practice

The form needs to include three main elements:

1   A review of past performance – from which lessons can be learnt. Also, to monitor results, skills, attributes and competencies.

2   A preview of the future – to plan for maintaining and improving future performance; agree actions, set objectives, standards and targets; identify development needs, support and training required.

3   An action planning session – action planning by the individual and manager to support implementation; a personal development plan, including support, training and development.

Grading staff, discussing performance

Question
"Our form *starts* with tick boxes, rating people on performance factors which affect bonus calculations. Discussions tend to centre on grading expectations and can get acrimonious if we disagree. The whole purpose of the interview gets hijacked. How can you grade staff *before* discussing their performance against objectives, key tasks, standards and targets?"

Making best use of the forms

Whatever the form's content and order, the manager has the discretion and flexibility to make the best use of it. The solution is to follow the dependency sequence structure agenda, as outlined in chapter 16 (p. 115).

Since all the agenda items should be included or implied in appraisal forms, managers can be *flexible* and discuss them in a *logical* order. Any ratings required are based on the *evidence of the performance and results already discussed, and agreed.*

Gaining self-assessment and agreement

First ask the individual to assess their performance against the criteria, and then to rate it based on examples. You then know how they rate themselves.

They may be:

- **Realistic** – your views coincide.
- **Harder on themselves** – it's less damaging for them to tell you about underperformance, than for you to tell them.
- **Unrealistic in terms of grading** – ask them for specific examples to justify their view (there may be information you are unaware of). If not, in light of the evidence, suggest they reassess their rating.

Ultimately, the decision is the manager's, based on *valid evidence.*

Limitations of ratings systems

Rating systems can be prescriptive and limiting with insufficient boxes to show enough detail or to encourage adequate discussion of performance, for example:

Below requirements ☐	Meets requirements ☐	Exceeds requirements ☐

The tendency is to go for the middle ground; people can feel pigeon-holed.

To counter this, a visual scale can help individuals and managers identify and discuss *performance* against *objectives* and *behaviours*.

Performance review and planning agreement

These scales have been developed to open up joint discussions on:

- What you achieved – the outputs of your performance objectives, eg numerically.

- How you achieved it – the behaviour and effort demonstrated during the year, eg delighted customers.

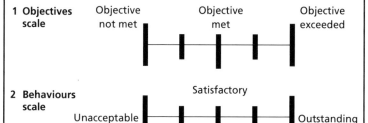

The scales help to clarify how you are working. Please respond honestly. Your manager has been asked to discuss with you how your responses reflect their understanding of your performance. To help you both come to an agreement, it is important to identify examples of your work which you believe support your evaluation.

During preparation, both managers and staff evaluate how far the objectives, priorities and targets have been met in *each* area. They mark the scales to identify this and use this information to open up discussion both on areas of convergence and divergence; to identify actual evidence and supporting examples, to reach a joint conclusion.

Because the scale is unnumbered, it is more comfortable for individuals to identify their position and discuss improvements.

If your forms have prescriptive tick boxes or labelling, you could use this simple scale as described. Only *after* this discussion are both managers and staff in a position to rate performance and competencies, based on the evidence.

Imprecise ratings

Question
"Our form rates people as follows: **1** Excellent **2** Exceeds requirements **3** Meets requirements **4** Below requirements. Most people get number 3. However, there is no way of differentiating whether they *just* 'meet requirements' or are almost into 'exceeds requirements'. There is little room to write comments and evidence to validate the ratings. How do I cope?"

Possible solutions
Three to five options can be prescriptive. They can usefully be opened out on an evaluation scale of 1–10 showing a more detailed differentiation of performance levels in objectives, key result areas and targets (this can be particularly valuable in relation to performance-related pay). Individuals can then evaluate their position more accurately. This can be used to

focus and motivate them to improve performance by identifying *how* (see example overleaf). If there is little room on forms for examples and evidence, number the items and write the additional information on a separate sheet.

Measuring performance through objectives, standards and targets

A key management requirement is the ability to motivate, develop and measure staff performance by setting objectives, standards and targets. This relies on four key elements:

1 Defining objectives

2 Identifying key result areas from them

3 Setting performance standards

4 Setting targets

} Against them

Four key elements

1 Objectives

Objectives are motivational and challenging goals that provide a sense of direction and focus. The end result required determines the course of action. Objectives can be set either for the job (an overall statement of the purpose and role, linked to outcomes), individually, or both.

Objectives, standards and targets should be 'SMART':

Example

PERFORMANCE REVIEW

Key result areas/tasks	EVALUATION SCALE									
	1	2	3	4	5	6	7	8	9	10
1										
2										
3										
4										
5										
6										
7										
8										
3 Boxes	1–3 Below requirements			4–7 Meets requirements				8–10 Exceeds requirements		
4 Boxes	1–3 Below requirements			4–7 Meets requirements				8–9 Exceeds requirements		10 Excellent
5 Boxes	1 Well below	2–3 Just below		4–7 Meets requirements				8–9 Exceeds requirements		10 Excellent

- **S**pecific.
- **M**easurable.
- **A**chievable, agreed.
- **R**ecognisable, relevant.
- **T**ime-bound.

When preparing objectives, standards and targets, make sure you:

- Write them in the form of short phrases or sentences, using verbs.
- Specify precisely the input, output, desired action or outcome.
- Are specific through the use of nouns or numbers in any form. Make them time-bound.
- Phrase them briefly and unambiguously.

2 Identifying key result areas

Key result areas are the key tasks and responsibilities which *must* be carried out in order to meet the objectives.

Example

> ### Administrative assistant
> **Objective** – to assist the manager by providing an effective administration service at all times.
>
> **Key result areas (only four listed)**
>
> 1 Dealing with all correspondence, paper or electronic.
> 2 Handling telephone enquiries.
> 3 Receiving callers.
> 4 Arranging meetings, recording the contents.

3 Setting performance standards

Performance standards are set for the *job*, and are therefore identical for each holder of the same job. They are a ruler, and define the minimum standards of performance in key result areas to meet the objectives.

Example

Administrative assistant

1 Dealing with all correspondence (only three shown)

- Electronic mail to be checked on an hourly basis.

- Receive and sort all mail, draw attention to urgent matters, by 10am.

- All paper correspondence to be date stamped, dealt with or acknowledged within two days of receipt.

Some jobs, for example sales, adapt well to measurable standards. Others may use recognisable methods of good practice, eg observing health and safety at work procedures.

Objectives, standards and targets are measurable in six ways:

1 Numerically – sales figures, productivity.

2 By deadline – meeting project dates, paper turn around.

3 Procedurally – adhering to quality or health and safety systems.

4 Financially – profitability, turnover, meeting budgets.

5 By feedback – positive or negative, number of recommendations, complaints or non-compliances.

6 Recognisable – house style, behavioural skills and attributes, eg customer focus.

Key result areas and standards

Again, it is good practice to write these in the form of short sentences, using plenty of verbs and deadlines. To achieve 'buy in', whenever possible set standards and targets through consultation with jobholders .

Key result area	Standards
Computer security	Confidential information on computer files must be permanently stored under relevant secure access codes by 10 April. Only designated individuals, authorised by directors, will have access to secure codes at all times.

4 Setting targets

Targets are set for *individuals*; they guage progress in achieving results and encourage self-assessment. Targets should motivate by being challenging, but realistic.

Targets are:

- Specific, measurable, timed future actions or results based on an individual's current performance against standards, competencies or tasks.

- Part of the ongoing appraisal and review process to develop skills, knowledge and competencies.

- Concerned with prioritisation, productivity and profitability. They should tell people what is expected of them and provide a regular self-checking mechanism.

It is important not to have more than about six targets at any one time. By regularly reviewing progress, signing off targets when met and setting new ones, the system will remain relevant and ongoing. Targets are set to:

- Bring an individual's performance up to standard and aim for continued improvement.

- Motivate by addressing areas in addition to routine work about priorities, change, special projects and developing potential.

- Monitor and improve communication and feedback between managers and staff.

Standards may be included in the job description, or written separately. It is essential to see how they relate to *key result areas and targets*, particularly during discussions at appraisal and reviews (see example opposite.)

Summary checklist

✓ Remember, managers have flexibility about the order in which forms are completed.

✓ Follow a logical agenda – discuss performance, key results, standards and targets *before* gradings.

✓ Gain self-appraisal against standards, targets, competencies and ratings.

✓ Set 'SMART' objectives, standards and targets by consultation.

Examples of key result areas, standards and targets

KEY RESULT AREAS Key tasks, responsibilities	STANDARDS OF PERFORMANCE To what minimum standard must each task be completed to fulfil the objectives?	TARGETS (*with deadlines*) About meeting standards, priorities, change, development, special projects
Personal assistant Job applications	All applications to be date stamped on arrival, and acknowledged within three working days	Clear backlog by 25 May Thereafter, all acknowledgements to be sent within the specified deadline
Sales consultant Developing new prospects	Identify and qualify against criteria ten new leads per month and telephone to make appointments	To achieve an average of three appointments per month from these ten leads
Administrator Ordering consumables	Stationery – check stock computer records daily Re-order designated amount when stock figures are orange	To have all types of stationery in stock 100% of the time over the next six months
Telephonist Answering incoming calls: Speed of response Public relations First impression helpful	Smile, sound welcoming Answer 90% of calls within three rings Give a greeting, "Good morning/afternoon", then the company name Speak clearly, ask "How may I help you?"	To answer 90% of calls to standard, within three rings, by 30 June Monitored by recordings and call counter

Managing reward – performance-related pay

This chapter covers:
> Identifying different types of schemes.
> The main intention; relating salary and performance.
> The importance of keeping the salary review and the appraisal system separate.

Research shows that about half of organisations with performance management systems use some method of relating pay to performance.

This varies widely, from pay on a commission-only basis to reward elements such as bonuses, commission and piece rates as well as profit or performance-related pay.

Different types of schemes

Some of the main ways in which performance-related pay is organised are:

- The overall rating determines *total* staff pay increases, related to their performance/competency level.

- Performance-related pay forms *part* of a pay increase.
- The scheme is related partly or wholly to profitability.
- The rating is linked to a bonus, rather than a salary increase, so one year's good performance is not reflected in an increase over time.

Case study

A company with performance-related pay linked to total salary got into a loss-making situation and had to hold down pay. Staff were working exceptionally hard to ensure company and job survival.

After the appraisal, managers were told to go back and deliberately under-mark performance. Too many staff were meeting or exceeding requirements and qualifying for a rise, which the company could not meet.

This caused great resentment. No matter how well staff performed it could not be fully acknowledged because of the pay implications.

The main intentions of aligning salary and performance

The main intentions of aligning salary and performance are:

- To match reward to an individual's contribution and results as accurately as possible.

- To redress any disparity between an individual's contribution and their salary (eg, people being recruited at different points of a salary scale).

- To encourage development in the current job, rather than always by promotion.

The challenge faced by organisations is to devise an objective, fair system to measure performance (preferably through consultation), then to align it to whatever type of reward system has been decided upon. Also, to communicate to all staff how the system works, and how it *benefits them.*

The challenge faced by managers is that, for most people, money is an incentive. However, by no means is it the only motivating factor. Whatever systems organisations adopt, managers have to implement the process in the fairest and most motivational way possible.

Managing a performance-related pay scheme

Effective procedures include:

- A clear explanation of the objectives and factors that contribute to salary review.

- Some guidance for managers on criteria and financial range.

- A proposal for the rise by the immediate boss.

- Examining the effect of the rise on the overall pattern of salaries in the organisation and department.

- A face-to-face explanation of the rise by the manager.

- Clear explanation of, and access to, the grievance procedure.

The salary review and appraisal

As far as possible, you need to keep the salary review process and the appraisal separate. They should be two quite distinct processes, dealt with at separate times.

Salary review

- A salary review looks at past performance to calculate its worth.
- The pay rise or bonus is recognition of this past performance.
- It is backward-focused.

Past performance

Performance appraisal

- The main focus is previewing future performance, in the light of lessons learnt.
- Agreeing actions, setting targets, planning the training and development route.
- It is forward-focused.

Future performance

With annual appraisals, ideally the salary review should take place six months later. This encourages the maximum effort, since when standards and targets are set staff know that their next six months' performance will be a factor when considering their pay rise. With six monthly appraisals, the pay review process should happen three months after an appraisal.

The difficulties of a linked appraisal and pay scheme

Question

"With our system the overall ratings decided on the year's performance determine staff pay, on an incremental scale. The rise becomes apparent at the appraisal and comes into effect two months later. Staff are unwilling to be open and admit or discuss underperformance or training needs because of pay implications. The appraisal becomes a pay bargaining interview. Very little relates to the future, it undermines relationships and honest communication. What can we do?"

Possible solutions

Managers need to:

- Feed back to *their* managers and HR department the problems and implications they encountered with the system, and share solutions.

- Clarify the appraisal process with staff to review performance, identify training needs and plan future actions.

- Discuss performance, training needs and action planning *before ratings.* Do this by making use of the dependency sequence agenda (see p. 115), and the ideas on talking about performance and gaining self-assessment outlined in chapter 8.

- Stress that the increase is merely a *part* of what people are worth, reflected in their whole salary package.

Summary checklist

✓ The complexity of reward-based schemes means that they need to be well researched and planned, through consultation.

✓ There must be a clear understanding of the purpose of the reward scheme, and how it relates to the appraisal process.

✓ This involves identifying the type of contribution to be rewarded, and the criteria for rewarding it.

✓ Schemes are most successful when implemented for a trial period, with opportunities to make necessary adjustments.

✓ Schemes work best in areas where the outputs and results are clearly definable through well thought out objectives, standards, competencies and target*s, which must be quantifiable and measurable*. Also, they should be set through consultation, be relevant and agreed, so the reward element is seen as fair.

✓ There should be maximum de-linkage possible between appraisal and salary review, or the purpose of the appraisal becomes subverted.

10

The manager's attitude and approach

This chapter considers:
> The objectives and purpose of appraisal.
> The attitudes staff and managers bring to appraisals.
> The implications of appraisal.
> The skill of appraising performance, *not* personality.
> Behaviour – listening and motivating.

Objectives of appraisal

As a manager your attitude towards the appraisal process is critical. Ask yourself why you are putting yourself through all the extra work, form filling, conflict and stress appraisal involves? Just because the company says so? Or, like climbing Mount Everest, just because it's there?

Check your motivation towards the appraisal process. Remember, appraisal is *not*:

- For blaming, point scoring and undermining.
- A general whingeing session.

- A disciplinary interview.
- A pay-bargaining session.

Appraisal *is*:

- A review of past performance, to learn from.
- A preview of the future, to identify objectives, needs and required outcomes.
- An action-planning session to map out actions required, targets and deadlines. Also, how to achieve this through support, training and development.

We cannot change the past, however, we *can* use it as a learning experience to influence the future. Therefore, the major focus in appraisal needs to be on *future performance, actions and development.*

So what are a manager's objectives in appraising staff performance? They generally fall into two categories, to do with improving *results* and *relationships.*

Appraisal objectives – best practice

- To achieve specific results and continuous improvement.
- To increase staff motivation to give their best.
- To develop skills, abilities, knowledge, responsibility and self-awareness.
- To produce a challenge, a sense of achievement, fun!
- To improve communication and the relationship between managers and staff.

Which of these objectives applies to you, in relation to your staff?

The attitudes staff and managers bring to appraisals

It is also worth considering the attitudes both managers and staff may bring to the appraisal process – often these are based on previous appraisal experiences, good, bad or indifferent.

For example, you or your staff may feel:

- "It's a waste of time, all these promises, nothing ever happens."

- "It's mainly to do with the past, all written beforehand. They don't listen, nothing you say makes much difference."

- "It's their chance to bring up all the year's mistakes, things they didn't mention at the time."

- "We set these objectives and targets and don't discuss them until the next appraisal; it's all pretty irrelevant then."

As a manager you may feel:

- "It's the dreaded appraisal time again. All those forms to fill in and boxes to tick. I can't remember what my staff were doing last month, let alone nine or ten months ago."

- "It's fine in theory, but I just haven't got time to do this preparation. With my staff, it takes all my time just getting the job done."

- "Why didn't I make any notes of those problems and dates, and deal with them at the time? I'm going to have to mention them now, because of the pay implications."

- "Look at this training and development plan. I had to cancel the training course and supervisory secondment because of staffing levels. I never got round to the coaching I kept promising."

If, on the other hand, you see appraisal as an opportunity, something you look forward to, you or your staff may feel:

- "I think it's a brilliant opportunity to have some of my manager's time, to be listened to, review what has happened and learn from it. To set objectives together, discuss realistic targets, plan how to get there, and then explore what support I need."

As a manager you may feel:

- "This is my opportunity to give some quality time to Sam, and listen. To offer recognition and praise for his attitude and hard work. To explore our concerns, see what we can learn. To recognise skills gaps, such as interpersonal skills, which affect relationships and are causing some problems with the team, and customers. So I'll need to plan support and training to improve these areas and develop Sam for the supervisory role."

The implications of appraisal

It is important that managers consider the implications of appraisal:

- The employee's performance and development are a partnership between the appraiser and appraisee.
- It is in the interest of the appraiser to appraise fairly and well, since appraisal is testing the manager's effectiveness in managing and developing staff.
- How appraisals have been handled, and the outcomes (including ongoing staff support and development), will form part of the manager's own appraisal.

It also greatly helps the attitude of staff if these implications are shared as part of their preparation. Remember, your attitude as a manager will be transmitted to staff, therefore you are largely responsible for the attitude staff have towards their appraisals.

The performance management concept

At the core of this concept lies a key idea, which managers need to understand – the difference between an individual's *personality* and their *behaviour*.

Personality – a person's own distinctive personal characteristics. What they are (which you cannot change).

Behaviour – everything they say or do; their approach/the way they treat others (which you can change).

Ask yourself: "How much can I change an individual's personality by appraising them?"

You need to separate the *personality characteristics* from the *behaviour/results*, and to concentrate on the part you *can* influence. Where there are difficulties with individuals, since you cannot change their personal characteristics, you need to look for a change in behaviour and performance.

Behaviour

Our behaviour is everything we say and do.

- It is learnt.
- Therefore we have a *choice* about how we behave.
- It is not something we are born with, like the colour of our eyes, or our height.
- It is something we choose, like the clothes we wear.
- Others can influence our behaviour, however, ultimately the choice is ours.

Remember, through your approach and behaviour to staff, you largely prime and prompt responses. Behaviour breeds behaviour.

We can all identify behaviours we would like to encourage and develop in our staff, and those we wish to discourage! And they can probably do the same with us. The ability to appraise performance *not* personality is a fundamental tenet of performance appraisal.

Motivating others

Strokes

As human beings we all have an innate need for positive 'strokes'; in the context of appraisal these take the form of acknowledgement, affirmation, recognition, thanks and praise. They can be both verbal and non-verbal. For example, listening actively and responding by looking at the person, having eye contact, nodding, leaning slightly forward, showing interest (non-verbal). Or acknowledging, questioning, clarifying, summarising, giving recognition, thanks or praise when appropriate (verbal), eg "Your good time keeping and willingness to stay and get the job done has set a example to the rest of the team. It's also encouraged them to do the same, thanks Alex".

The ability to give positive strokes to staff is not a skill which comes to most managers naturally. Much depends on managers' role models and personal experience of receiving strokes. If, as a manager, you have been motivated by receiving recognition and praise, then you are more likely to do the same. You need to be aware of this behaviour and its importance as a motivational factor. You also need to know how to give appropriate and valid praise (based on behaviour/results) without embarrassment.

Summary checklist

✓ It is important to have a positive attitude towards appraisal; remember, your attitude as a manager largely determines staff attitudes.

✓ Appraise *performance* not personality.

✓ Remember, you have a choice about how you behave.

✓ Motivate others through strokes, recognition and praise.

The skills of appraisal interviewing

This chapter offers advice on:
> Questioning skills.
> Active listening, acknowledging and showing empathy.
> Clarifying and summarising.
> Confirming, getting agreement and commitment.
> Body language, signalling and signposting.

Questioning techniques

Managers need to be experts in a variety of interpersonal skills at appraisals. Questions are the key to unlocking information, controlling or closing conversations. However, it all depends which ones you use. It's not knowing the right answer that counts, it's knowing the right question!

The 'right' question in many cases is 'open specific', used to draw out a particular piece of information rather than a straight 'yes' or 'no' answer. However, managers need to use many types of questions to become skilled appraisers.

Main types of questions

- **Open** – these begin with 'What', 'Where', 'When', 'Why', 'Which', 'Who', 'How' and 'Tell me...', eg "Who supervises Sally?

These questions elicit information, not a straight yes or no.

- **Closed** – these elicit yes/no answers, eg "Have you told John?"

- **Specific** – these can be open or closed. They specify the information required through the use of nouns or numbers, eg "How many staff do you manage?"

- **Leading** – these have the answer implied in the question, eg "I expect you support the merger?"

- **Behavioural** – these seek examples of behaviour, eg "What has been the most difficult complaint you have received recently?" Listen, followed by "How did you handle it?"

- **Hypothetical** – a 'What if' question, eg "If you are promoted, how will you deal with Ann's timekeeping problem?"

- **Reflective** – reflects the information back to the giver in a statement, to get them to open up on attitudes and feelings. For example, the appraisee says "I didn't have a very good relationship with Jason." (Reflected back) – "You feel you didn't get on very well with Jason?" Pause, wait for them to reflect and elaborate.

It is essential to understand, plan and list the right questions needed to explore topics and open up discussions.

Listening

There are three main barriers to effective listening:

1   Selective attention – we decide whether we are going to listen or not.

2 Selective interpretation – we decide how we interpret the information, *based on our perspective or agenda.*

3 Selective retention – we decide what to remember, based on what we interpret as important, to us.

Listening is a multi-functional activity. While we are 'listening' we may also be busy:

• Disagreeing.

• Thinking of the implications.

• Thinking of an answer.

• Thinking of the next question.

Before we can listen to anyone, we have to enter into a mental compact with ourselves to *really* listen.

Listening *actively* involves concentration and focus.

The key stages are:

1 Deciding to listen.

2 Pure listening – retaining information *without* interpretation.

3 Acknowledging – reflecting back what is said or felt.

4 Clarifying – statements or questions to show understanding of the *implications.*

5 Summarising – facts, situations, agreements, disagreements or actions.

6 Understanding then takes place.

7 A considered response – only possible *after* the other stages.

Use of pauses and silence

Pauses allow the listener time to assimilate information, reflect and format a reply. The more complex the information, the longer the time required.

Ask a question then remain silent – to probe and gain information and feelings.

Other barriers to listening

- Information presented in a confusing, contradictory way.

- Interference – noise, being interrupted or talked over.

- Blockages – mental blocks; the speaker's manner or personality. Not paying attention (because it's *not* what we want to hear). We 'switch off' and stop listening.

To aid active listening use statements and summaries. Statements feed in additional facts to clarify misunderstandings, "So what you are saying is...", or to give information where needed, to create understanding.

When disagreeing with someone, acknowledge their right to that point of view, summarise their point(s) before using 'however' and presenting your position. "I understand why you feel so annoyed, because this is the third time it's happened. However, I ..."

Summaries – interim and final

Interim – keep control of the conversation. Mark the progress and achievements so far.

Final – give a positive finish, sum up the achievements and agreements. Confirm future actions, and get commitment. "Right, so you agree you will organise coaching for Sue within three weeks, let's put that down as an action point."

It is the *listener* who controls the conversation. Concentrate throughout, analyse what is or isn't said, and its significance. Pick up points for expansion. Notice discrepancies or generalisations that may need questioning specifically.

To be a good appraiser, you need to do at least twice as much listening as talking.

Body language

A considerable part of what we say is communicated non-verbally, particularly if we are feeling nervous and are therefore 'incongruent' (saying one thing while our body language 'says' another).

Positive non-verbal communication

- Smile, look welcoming.
- Sit so you can see and be seen; avoid being behind a desk.
- Have regular, comfortable eye contact.
- Avoid constant note taking and distracting gestures.
- Cultivate an open, interested and encouraging expression.
- Avoid frowning if the appraisee says something negative about themselves as this may inhibit disclosure.

Signalling

We signal constantly with our body language. Through the 'open hand' gesture we invite staff to take a seat, or encourage them to speak. Actions that can send negative signals include pen or foot tapping and pointing. We can consciously use positive signals like smiling a welcome and extending a warm handshake to put the appraisee at ease; looking relaxed, to help relax them. Humour is also a great tension breaker.

Signposting

Signposting is done verbally to point the way ahead. It helps to outline the plan – what's going to happen – and timescales. For example, in the introduction indicate the interview's purpose, plan and timescale – "I've set aside between one to one and a half hours for our interview, so there's plenty of time to discuss things"; "Congratulations on the way you handled that Jean. Now I would like to move on and look at the next key result area ..."; "We've got about 15 minutes left, so we need to be completing our action planning."

Signposting makes the appraisee feel secure; they know where they are, where they are going, and how much longer they've got.

Summary checklist

✓ It is essential to plan *the right* questions to open up discussion and elicit specific answers.

✓ *Decide* to listen, acknowledge, clarify, summarise and understand *before* responding.

✓ Monitor body language to give positive messages. Smile, look open and relaxed.

✓ Use signalling and signposting to give security; tell people where they are, and where they're going.

Giving feedback

> This chapter considers:
> > Criticism and feedback – what is the difference?
> > What is the purpose of feedback?
> > Giving feedback in positive and negative situations.
> > Different feedback styles and their uses.

Giving relevant feedback, objectively and positively, is one of the key skills of conducting effective appraisals. It relates back to the concept of appraising *performance*, not personality.

Feedback deals with behaviour – which the individual can change – *not* their personal characteristics.

Criticism and feedback

There is often confusion about the meaning of criticism and feedback. A dictionary definition of criticism includes 'A remark pointing out a fault'; 'To examine critically' and 'To express a judgement about'.

No wonder people react so badly when criticism is mentioned or implied. There is, of course, *positive* criticism, eg "You handled that discussion really well" (just praise).

However, as a manager you need something more relevant and powerful – *feedback*.

	Destructive criticism	Constructive feedback
1	Focuses on personality and attitude	Concentrates on behaviour and results
2	Is often impulsive/ emotional	Is planned, uses specific examples
3	Focuses on the problem	Focuses on positive solutions
4	Is often critical and judgemental	Is depersonalised, non-judgemental
5	Damages relationships	Builds trust, strengthens relationships

Feedback

What is feedback?

Feedback is a mirror; reflecting back to the giver information about, and examples of, their behaviour and how this affects others. It also offers suggestions and advice.

If an individual is under-achieving or acting inappropriately, and is unaware of this, *not telling them denies them the opportunity to take action*. Sharing information shows your belief and confidence in their ability to act, and their potential to develop.

Purpose

Feedback is a learning opportunity to help someone improve by:

- Being aware of *what* they say and do.
- *How* they do it – their manner and attitude.
- *How* this affects others – cause and effect.
- *How* they can achieve the optimum outcome.

Feedback leaves the individual free to accept this information and make use of it, if the giver *avoids* evaluative, critical or judgemental language, eg "If only you had the common sense to tell me Ann was off sick, this problem wouldn't have happened." Instead, the person giving the feedback should depersonalise the message and concentrate on *future* behaviour, eg "In future, if Ann's away let me know at once so we can prevent problems." This avoids blaming or judgements about the individual's personal characteristics and attitudes.

Negative feedback

Sometimes managers have to give feedback when things are not going well. They often find this difficult, for fear of harming relationships. They also may lack the skills to feed back positively and constructively.

Giving feedback in negative situations

- First find something positive to acknowledge – perhaps relating to another area.
- Introduce the subject under discussion.
- Identify the behaviour being reviewed – use specific examples and factual evidence.

- Ask the appraisee to explain the impact of the behaviour – help the individual to realise the consequences of their behaviour.

- Seek a solution – ask for options and solutions; confirm right answers or offer suggestions.

- Agree the required solution and outcome – agree specifically the actions required; check and confirm commitment to action.

Receiving negative feedback

- It is easy to slip into a defensive mode when receiving negative feedback; try and keep your body language open.

- Concentrate; listen to the individual giving feedback. Listen actively, by acknowledging.

- Reflect back the feedback – check that you have understood the information correctly.

- Clarify the feedback – request specific examples; ask questions.

- Offer and discuss options and solutions. Finally, ask the appraisee for suggestions and options.

Positive feedback

Giving positive feedback reinforces correct decisions, actions and behaviour. It builds confidence and motivates staff 'to do the same again'.

Giving positive feedback

- Introduce the subject under discussion – begin on a note of praise.

- Identify positive behaviours – use specific information and concrete, behavioural examples as evidence.

- Ask and confirm the impact of the behaviour – help the individual to see the benefits of the behaviour.

- Reinforce continued use of the behaviour – related to needs and benefits.

Different styles of feedback

There are four different styles of feedback – they are described and illustrated below.

Example

A sales presentation

1 "That presentation didn't go very well. You don't seem to have taken in much product knowledge. You need to show real improvement George."
Style 1 – critical, negative, non-specific.

2 "You handled that presentation really well Ann."
Style 2 – positive praise, non-specific, subjective (the giver's opinion). It left the receiver *guessing* what they had done right.

3   "That presentation went really well because you had planned it with the customers' needs in mind. First, you caught their attention by asking relevant questions about their problems. Then you demonstrated how our product would provide a cost-effective solution. You allowed time for questions and summed up confirming the benefits to them. Congratulations on the order James."

   Style 3 – positive, specific, work-related, reinforcing feedback. The manager gave clear, reinforcing examples of positive behaviour and results, encouraging the same behaviour again.

4   Mary's presentation got off to a difficult start because of an unresolved problem.

   "We need to evaluate carefully what happened Mary, to learn from it. At the beginning of the presentation you were talking a lot about the software and its capabilities. The customer wasn't listening, all he was interested in was the fact that the previous programme was faulty. So let's go back to the beginning when Tim fired those questions at you. What could you have done to calm him down? How else could you have handled the situation? How might that have changed the outcome? If you ever find yourself in a similar situation, how would you handle it?"

   Style 4 – empathetic feedback that was positive, specific, factual, non-judgemental and developmental. This enabled Mary, through questions, to self-assess the situation, without feeling too defensive. A hypothetical question was then used to see if and what Mary had learnt from the situation. This last style is known as *developmental feedback*.

Consider which style is going to benefit you and your staff most.

Summary checklist

✓ Destructive criticism is focused on personality and attitude.

✓ Constructive feedback is information based on behaviour and results, giving specific examples to reinforce positive behaviour.

✓ Constructive feedback flags up negative behaviour and consequences, and offers positive solutions and advice.

✓ Feedback is depersonalised and non-judgemental; it aims to bring about positive results through insight.

The process of developmental feedback

> This chapter covers:
> > The concept, use and skills of developmental feedback.
> > How to receive and handle criticism.

When giving feedback in negative situations, being able to use *developmental feedback* is essential. Developmental feedback involves factually describing the situation, behaviour and results. It also involves asking open, specific, non-judgemental questions to enable the individual to self-assess and explore other options/ outcomes. This brings about insight (in terms of cause and effect), gives ownership to the receiver and avoids damaging working relationships.

 Case study

Bob has a supervisor, Karen, who is under a lot of time pressure at work. She tends to behave aggressively towards others, particularly if they come with bad news or a problem. Team

members have become reluctant to approach her with difficulties, which then become crises.

Bob felt unsure how to deal with the situation. He felt Karen would feel criticised, and would probably become defensive and aggressive with him. Bob discussed the situation with his manager, Tessa, whom he knew was skilled at handling feedback. She discussed situations with him, and asked questions that prompted Bob to analyse the situation and suggest most of the answers. Only then did she offer suggestions.

The coach concept

Let's look at this situation in a bit more detail. Tessa explained a key idea; she asked Bob for the qualities and actions of a good sports coach. Bob suggested that a good coach:

- Listens, observes.
- Explains if you get it right or wrong.
- Warns, makes suggestions, offers advice.
- Demonstrates the skills.
- Recognises effort, gives praise.
- Supports, encourages, motivates.

Through the use of questions, Tessa enabled Bob to realise that this was just the approach he needed to use with Karen. The coach concept – not a critic but a coach.

Using developmental feedback

Tessa offered to help Bob deal with Karen's situation. She explained the concept of developmental feedback and coached him to develop a series of questions which could help him discuss the situation with Karen, and enable her to self-assess and find a solution she would implement.

Tessa explained that when investigating a difficult incident, behaviour or attitude, it is useful to ask open, specific questions to explore the situation, an individual's behaviour and possible options.

Below are Bob's questions (Tessa's guidelines follow in brackets).

1 "When someone comes to you with a problem how do you tend to react?"

(Draw out *their attitude* to someone approaching them with a problem.)

2 "What do you do?"

(Get the person to identify their body language, and to monitor for signs of aggression, eg frowning, pointing fingers, invading personal body space.)

3 "What do you say?"

(**Content** – is it curt, blaming, lowering or judgemental, eg "If only you…"; "You should have…"; "It's your fault"?

Delivery of speech – what is their tone; is it cold, discouraging or critical? Is their voice raised, shouting? What about speed of delivery; is it fast and aggressive or slow and deliberate, perhaps threatening?)

4 "What is the *result* on the person who needs to approach you?"

(Encourage awareness of cause and effect. If this is habitual behaviour, draw out their *attitude* towards someone approaching them, and the *results*.)

5 "How likely are your team to approach you early, when there's a problem or something has changed?"

6 "How important is it that you get an early warning?"

7 "So what can you suggest to encourage people to come to you early, before things reach crisis point?"

Let's consider question 7 in more detail. For question 7, a positive response from Karen might be "I'll talk to them at the team meeting about the importance of flagging up problems early. Explain that I've been under a bit of pressure, may have over-reacted to bad news. That I'll make an effort to stay calm, focus on solving the problem rather than blaming them."

If the response lacks insight, ask more questions, eg "If you were flagging up a situation that could *prevent* future problems, how would *you* like to be treated?" Or "So what *actions* can *you* take to encourage an early approach, to prevent a crisis?"

If you are still unable to get appropriate answers, then ask more questions, eg "How do you think it would help if you raised the situation at the next team meeting, and discussed your future plans for handling bad news?" Or "So that people realise you are going to try and react differently in future, how useful would it be to explain this, and get their support?"

The questions are framed to draw out a *positive* response, so you can then confirm the right answers.

If you get "it would be a waste of time" go back to probing to uncover the reason(s) and attitude behind the answer, eg "What makes you say that?" Avoid asking 'Why' as it can sound judgemental.

Then you can work with the underlying issues, through questioning techniques.

Bringing about change

- Complete an action plan on the changes committed to by both parties.
- Set standards and deadlined targets.
- Book one-to-one meetings to review progress, regularly.

Results

A month later, after their next review, Bob asked Karen for some written feedback on progress, and how he had handled the situation. This was her response:

"The whole feedback process made me feel consulted, that my suggestions were valued and listened to. So now I'm trying to put them into practice. I feel my relationship with the team and you is better. When we communicate I don't feel so criticised, even about the difficult areas, like the effect I was having on my team. When you asked me for feedback about how you managed the situation, and how I felt, it made it a two-way process. I feel more positive about my job now, in spite of the pressures."

Receiving criticism

If in seeking feedback you receive criticism from a colleague, choose to use the *thinking* rather than the *emotional* side of your brain. Avoid a habitual response, being passive or submissive, or getting 'hooked' into the defence and attack syndrome. *Respond* don't react.

If true:

- Listen and acknowledge.
- Admit you got it wrong.
- Apologise for the situation caused.
- Consult with the individual(s) to problem solve.
- Work on resolving the situation.
- Meet, review progress/preventative action.

If untrue:

- Listen and acknowledge.
- Show you can see how the misunderstanding arose.
- Say that it's not true, and why.

If partly true:

- Listen, acknowledge.
- State what is true.
- State what is *not* true, and briefly explain why.
- Consult, agree to work on the area that needs action.
- Meet, review the progress/solution.

Summary checklist

✓ Use the skills of developmental feedback when giving feedback in negative situations.

✓ Use the coach concept – understand which types of questions bring about self-appraisal and awareness of cause and effect.

✓ Handle criticism through listening, responding and acknowledging.

14

Conducting successful upwards and 360° appraisals

> This chapter covers:
> > Factors common to both systems.
> > Steps to conducting a successful upwards appraisal.
> > Useful questions to gain upwards feedback.
> > The process of completing a 360°appraisal.
> > Receiving 360° feedback.

The purpose and focus of both these systems has already been mentioned in chapter 5.

Factors common to both systems

- A requirement to have clear objectives and be carefully developed and planned.

- Are based on questionnaires (named or confidential); may be paper or computer-based.

- Information collected has to be collated, analysed and fed back cost effectively.

- Staff need to understand the system, be briefed on its objectives, methods and implementation.

- The process is dependent on the effectiveness of feedback. Individuals require skills to both *give and receive* feedback in positive and negative situations (see chapters 12 and 13).

- Decisions need to be made on how feedback will be presented and by whom. For reasons of impartiality a trained facilitator (internal or external) may be used.

- Individuals can then use this information to develop insight into how their actions and behaviour are perceived, and focus on the specific actions required to become more effective.

- Those receiving uncomfortable feedback may need help in coming to terms with issues previously unrecognised or denied.

- Both systems undoubtedly raise expectations of support and development. Demotivation will follow if adequate support and follow-up systems are not in place.

Upwards feedback

Although upwards feedback is sometimes informally sought by managers in traditional appraisal, it is now becoming more widely used in a formal system. Organisations are recognising the value of a more open, two-way dialogue that supports managers in seeking feedback from their staff. It is also increasingly recognised that staff are best placed to give feedback on a manager's performance.

A well organised, effective system helps to create a more informed, no-blame culture. Staff are seen as internal customers. They feel more consulted, involved, listened to, empowered and part of a team.

Conducting upwards appraisal

1 Familiarise yourself with all aspects of the scheme and how it is processed:

   a) Paperwork, guidelines.
   b) Objectives, questions or questionnaires, timing.
   c) Methods of collecting, collating, processing, feeding back and utilising information.

2 Brief your staff on upwards appraisal:

   a) Objectives – make sure they know that it is a mutual, fact-finding, non-judgemental process. Part of a no-blame, preventative culture.
   b) Explain that you will be asking for feedback on the way you process and organise work. Also on your skills, attitudes, behaviour as a manager, and what improvements you might make.

3 Brief on the scheme and its operation:

   a) How information will be used, and the benefits.

4 Thank staff for their contribution:

   a) Stress its value and benefits.

Questions

As a manager, you need to ask questions to get feedback about your staff's perceptions of your abilities, performance and attitude (which may be different from your own!)

For example, you may feel you are an excellent timekeeper while your staff wish you would consider the impact your decisions have on *their* timescales.

- "I would like to discuss the way work is organised and processed between us; what do I do that you find helpful?"
- "What processes would you like me to change or do differently to support you more?"
- "How does my time management affect your work?"
- "How did/does my attitude and behaviour affect our working relationship?"
- "If there were two things you could change about me, what would they be?"
- "How well do I communicate with you, orally and in writing?"
- "What areas should we focus on to help meet objectives over the next three months?"

Individuals should be encouraged to give *specific examples* of what the manager said or did, or could have done, in their feedback.

Case study

A company had what they perceived as a staff retention problem in two teams.

They introduced upwards appraisal via a questionnaire, but found that individuals were reluctant to give feedback on two rather aggressive managers. The forms had to be completed by hand, and were therefore attributable – feedback was minimal and bland.

Last year the company changed to using an online questionnaire, completed confidentially and e-mailed to HR. For the first time the feedback addressed the issues. When fed *back compositely, which prevented any scapegoating, it raised the awareness of the managers about how their behaviour and attitudes were affecting teamwork and morale.*

Because feedback was given to all managers by the personnel manager, the company became aware of the extent of the problem. Steps were taken to set standards of behaviour in the appropriate areas; to offer interpersonal skills and team-building training to the managers. The results and progress were monitored. Teamworking and morale on both teams improved considerably, as did staff retention.

Using and completing 360° appraisals

360° appraisals involve all-round feedback, from colleagues, internal and sometimes external customers. Consistent messages from several sources reinforce and confirm strengths, and make the denial of negative behaviour and actions difficult. You may complete 360° appraisals for colleagues, or generate them for others to give *you* feedback. This may be done through an independent facilitator.

The process

- The manager or HR department sends out the relevant paperwork, and colleagues, the team and customers are briefed about the purpose of the process and the need for objectivity when answering. Often a sample question and answer is given, to guide respondents, eg:

Question – what do I do that supports the team most?

Response (examples, behavioural evidence) – holding weekly team meetings, listening to our ideas/viewpoints. Prioritising and delegating tasks promptly. When James was away, planning immediately who would do his work, and doing part of it yourself.

- The information is collected, collated, analysed and fed back to the individual constructively.

- How it is used, implemented and supported will vary between organisations.

Completing a 360° form

This is your opportunity to give your *point of view* and *influence* the way things are done.

- Consider the purpose of the process and the objectivity required.

- Give responses in terms of specific examples and behavioural evidence.

- Be constructive and non-judgemental.

- Avoid negative criticism, eg "Ann didn't do X, so the deadline wasn't met."

- Use constructive feedback – "If in future Ann does X, the deadline could be met."

- Think "How will what I say *motivate* this person to make the changes I want?"

  (To motivate, it has to *benefit* them.) If the answer is "It won't", think of a way of expressing it that *will*!

Receiving 360° feedback

When receiving feedback, remember the objectives of the process:

- To provide information and insight into how you operate and are perceived by your 'customers' (internal *and* external).

- To use this information to improve your service and relationship with customers, to help release your full potential to meet your objectives more effectively.

How comfortable it feels to receive 360° feedback will largely depend on the skill of the giver, and your own level of *insight* into *your behaviour and actions (cause and effect)*.

Receiving feedback

- View 360° appraisal as a positive learning opportunity.

- Listen for affirmation and reinforcement of what is going well, to replicate it.

- Be prepared – you may receive uncomfortable information as well as comfortable.

- *Respond don't react* – slow down, avoid the defence-attack syndrome.

- In case you receive negative feedback, be familiar with, and prepared to use, the guidelines in chapter 12 (see p. 86).

- Use the information as a learning opportunity.

- If it is available, seek help in coming to terms with unrecognised or difficult issues.

Summary checklist

✓ Understand your system, the demands and benefits.

✓ Recognise that 360° feedback requires an open, supportive, no-blame culture to flourish.

✓ Use the opportunity to supply specific information in a non-critical or judgemental manner.

✓ Be prepared to use the information positively as a learning experience, and implement changes.

Conducting a successful competency-based appraisal

> This chapter covers:
> > Competency-based appraisals; examples, benefits.
> > Different competency formats and their uses.
> > Appraising competencies.

Competency-based appraisals enable organisations to be much more specific about what they expect in terms of behavioural skills, attributes and levels of competence from their staff.

What is a competency objective?

A competency objective is a statement which defines:

1   The skill, task or performance factor to be carried out.

2   The standards of performance/competence required, eg:

Competence – developing staff

- Reviews staff skills and training requirements, at least quarterly.

- Provides a timed personal development plan for staff coaching, training and mentoring.

- Provides opportunities to develop staff's capacity to handle increasingly complex work and responsibilities through job shadowing/sharing.
- Recognises and reinforces effective performance through regular acknowledgement, praise and thanks.
- Holds regular individual reviews (minimum three monthly) and annual appraisals.

A competency-based appraisal measures the presence or absence (and to what level) of the required competence, behavioural skill/attribute and performance factor. It does this by gaining:

- Factual supporting evidence – actual work examples of when this has or hasn't happened, and to what degree.
- Behavioural examples – eg showing consideration; he/she first considers the impact of their words and actions on others and their workloads.

Benefits of competency-based appraisals

- Consistency – all staff across the organisation work to the *same* definitions of the defined competence, which provides consistency.
- Clarity – the competence clearly defines the input required, giving behavioural examples and providing a common language to discuss performance.
- Focus – individuals know what they are required to do or need to focus on.
- Measurement – the competence provides a ruler for staff to self-appraise against and managers to measure with.

Organisations express competencies in many different formats. The three main types are listed, with examples:

1 The competence and performance standards required (see p. 104/5).

2 The competence is identified, with a list of both positive and negative indicators.

Competence – meeting targets

Positive – accepts ownership of targeted results, is focused on achieving them.

Negative – when targets are not met or mistakes are made, acts irresponsibly, blames others.

---

3 The competence is defined, with behavioural examples demonstrating competency levels, 1 being the highest.

Competence – self-confidence, expressing opinions	
Level	**Definition**
1	Regularly expresses ideas and opinions assertively and confidently.
2	Is willing to express ideas and opinions positively.
3	Will express ideas and opinions if they are sought.
4	Is sometimes able to express ideas and opinions, rather hesitantly.
5	Is unsure or reluctant about expressing ideas/opinions; does so submissively.

Individuals assess their level of competence and discuss how much it coincides with their manager's assessment.

Core and specialist competencies

Some organisations develop core competencies such as communicating, planning and organising, which apply to all staff. However, more senior staff are expected to achieve advanced levels of competence. Additional levels of competence might be required for senior managers and directors, eg customer focus, management:

- Demonstrates an overriding desire to meet customer needs, exceed their expectations by regular communication, seeking feedback on results and acting on it.

- Bases operational decisions on identified customer and business needs, and feedback.

Appraising competencies

- Make sure both you and your staff understand the objectives, system and guidelines.

- Ensure all managers and staff have copies of the forms/ competencies prior to the appraisal. Both managers and staff should independently assess the level of competence against the definition, based on facts and behavioural examples, identified to support their assessments.

- Performance and competence must always be discussed *before* conclusions are reached or grading agreed, particularly if there is an element of performance-related pay.

- Managers should *first* ask staff to discuss and describe their own levels of competence, and to identify actions, results and behavioural examples to illustrate their self-evaluation.

- If staff:

Under-rate their performance – this gives the manager the opportunity to acknowledge skills, contributions and build self-confidence. The manager must give *positive examples* of actions and results to validate the assessment and encourage repetition.

Over-estimate performance – the manager should ask for specific examples of behaviour and results to validate the staff's assessment, eg "Give me two specific examples of behaviour and results in relation to... which you consider constitutes evidence for your assessment."

If staff can produce evidence you were unaware of in line with the competency definition, you may alter your assessment. If not, you would *give examples of behaviour and skills which are required to meet the definition*. Gain agreement that they were not present to the required level and agree the assessment and grade.

- It is essential to record examples on the forms *as evidence on which the assessment/grade* has been agreed.

- Have plenty of open, specific questions ready to probe the competency performance levels in all required areas, eg, "Give me examples of actions which you consider demonstrate this level of competence in ..."; "How many of these actions did you take then?"; "So we can agree one key action was omitted, and therefore the competency was achieved to level two (or not fully achieved?)"

As a manager, your task is to bring your staff to a *realistic assessment* of their *actual competence* against the definition in order to gain agreement on assessment levels and therefore, if relevant, grading and pay implications.

Competency systems – pay-related

If your system is pay-related, and the rise is disclosed at appraisal, always make sure you are fully aware of staff performance in all the competencies, with examples. Also, discuss performance and competency levels first since the rise must be related to competency levels to be fair.

Summary checklist

✔ Ensure both you and your staff understand the objectives, systems, guidelines and use of competencies.

✔ Discuss performance and competence before agreeing any assessment or grading.

✔ Ask staff to discuss their own levels of competence *first*.

Preparation, process and implementation of appraisal

This chapter covers:
> Preparation steps – both manager's and staff's.
> The pre-meeting – purpose, agenda, paperwork.
> The process – the manager's preparation for appraisal.
> Conducting the appraisal – the agenda.
> Implementation – through personal development plans and reviews.

Preparation

Good preparation for appraisal is an investment in the future performance and success of your staff, and therefore of yourself. Hence the importance of following these guidelines, appropriate for all types of appraisal, and allowing adequate planning and preparation time for all parties.

Guidelines

Job descriptions

You need to review job descriptions (preferably through consultation), making sure they are up-to-date and relevant. Synchronise diaries, book dates and times for the preparation pre-meeting and the appraisal – book a neutral room if possible. Consider the preparation time required.

Pre-meeting – helping the appraisee prepare

The pre-meeting is particularly important if the system has changed, or you have not appraised a particular individual before. It is *essential* to know what their previous appraisal experience has been, and what their expectations are. These may be very high if they have received motivational appraisals previously. However, if the opposite is true, they may well be cynical or apprehensive. With 360° appraisal, pre-meetings may be required with all the parties concerned.

Not holding a pre-meeting can give away a great deal about the priority a manager puts on appraisal, so can cancelling without good reason.

The appraisee's attitude to the process is the manager's responsibility.

The main objectives of the pre-meeting are to:

- Brief staff on the objectives, system, process and your approach.
- Motivate staff; deal with any concerns.
- Encourage and help staff to prepare.

Pre-meeting agenda

- Explain the purpose and agenda of the pre-meeting.
- Sell the benefits and opportunities of appraisal.
- Allay concerns, tackle cynicism; overcome any previous poor appraisal experiences.
- Give the relevant paperwork and guidance notes, discuss, answer questions.
- Encourage and help the appraisee to prepare.
- Gain commitment to the process.
- Advise the date, time and venue of the appraisal, if not already agreed.

Paperwork for the appraisee's preparation (as applicable or available)

- The job description.
- The last appraisal form.
- One-to-one reviews.
- The previous period's objectives, key result areas, standards, targets, competencies and service-level agreements.
- A blank copy of the appraisal form and guidance notes.
- Appraisal agenda and questions.
- Previous training and development plan.
- Any other paperwork specific to your system.
- For 180° or 360° appraisal, the questionnaire.

Encourage the appraisee to talk to others they have working relationships with to get feedback and prepare thoroughly.

Managers with a number of staff sometimes hold a joint briefing meeting, although they should always speak with everyone personally to handle individual issues.

In situations where staff are geographically dispersed, briefing and support may sometimes have to be done via the intranet and telephone.

The manager's preparation

As part of effective preparation managers need to consider and do the following:

1 Review:

- The job description
- Previous appraisal form } If available
- One-to-one reviews for previous period

2 Consider the last period's:

- Objectives.
- Key result areas.
- Performance standards, competencies or service agreements.
- Targets.
- Also consider the appraisee's other working relationships, gather feedback. Also, the individual's, departmental and organisational needs.
- Be aware of the appraisee's results, achievements and new qualifications. Also, any training and development plan; commitments met or not met.

3 Anticipate:

- Areas of concern, questions and aspirations.

4 Complete appraisal form

- Your understanding of an individual's performance, with examples and evidence, using bulletpoints.

5 Consider development and training needs, and how to achieve these:

- Job-sharing, shadowing, job swap, secondment.
- Coaching, on-the-job training.
- Self-managed and e-learning, training courses (don't forget to check the availability of training budget funds!)

If appropriate:

- Were training commitments for the last period met? (If not, why not, and how should you handle this?)
- Is training required for 180° or 360° appraisal, in giving and receiving feedback?

6 Consider next year's:

- Objectives, key result areas, standards and competencies.
- Changes desired, constraints and potential targets.

7 Plan, prepare and hold the pre-meeting

- This is particularly important if the system or staff have changed.

Holding the appraisal

The welcome and introduction set the scene and *reveal the manager's attitude* to the process.

Initial welcome

To create empathy, use a smile, handshake and some relevant 'ice breaker' comment, often not work-related.

The introduction

This covers the appraisal purpose, plan, timing and note-taking.

Achievements

It's great to start on a note of recognition, acknowledgement of constraints or praise. "Congratulations on getting the Ward project done on time, especially with the specification changes." However, be careful not to pre-empt what the appraisee may want to say, for example, if you follow up the above comment with "What has given you the greatest satisfaction during the last year?" the answer is likely to be "The Ward project"! It is best to start with a credit balance first, as people are then more willing to discuss any debits.

Then open up the discussion, following this dependency sequence structure (if your form differs).

Agenda

1   Welcome and introduction – the purpose of the appraisal, plan, timing, mutual note taking, praise.

2   General discussion of the period under review, overall objectives.

3   Key result areas – appraisee's performance in each

4   Achievements and strengths   } Their opinion *then yours*

5   Areas of performance that could be improved

6   General concerns and problems facing you both in the organisation; how they were handled.

7   Consideration of last period's objectives, standards, competencies and targets.

   a) Agree assessment. If applicable, complete ratings against these results

   b) Discuss and outline new ones for the next period.

8   The future – the appraisee's support, training and development needs.

9   Action planning, showing commitments and deadlines *by both parties* to enhance performance and meet objectives.

10 Book date for the next review meeting.

The interview

This is an opportunity for relaxed, extended, structured conversation, taking an overview of the whole period. From the information reviewed, both the manager and the appraisee will have prepared draft copies of the appraisal form, using bullet points, giving examples and valid evidence. Then the interview will be focused, accurate and shorter, because the groundwork has been done.

Through the use of 'open' questions appraisees should be encouraged to give examples and evidence; to do *at least* two thirds of the talking. The manager asks for the appraisee's perceptions *first* to gain self-appraisal. Both parties can then discuss how the appraisee's responses reflect or diverge from the manager's understanding of the performance and results, and why. Both parties can then usually reach a consensus.

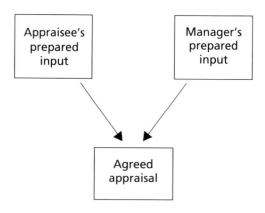

Personal development plans

During the appraisal, training and development needs will be identified, recorded, and put in a personal development plan file given to the individual. This contains copies of reviews, appraisals, qualifications and all developmental activities.

This plan acts as a motivator, giving the individual ownership of their personal development. At reviews, staff can remind the manager of commitments made and push for their implementation. (See overleaf for an example of a personal development plan.)

Monitoring

The manager's boss will normally review the appraisal, since how it has been managed and the outcomes should form part of the manager's own appraisal.

Personal development plan

Name		Position(s)		Department/Team		Date	
Topic	Developmental need		Proposed method		Action by (person) (date)		

Appeal

If the appraisee and manager strongly disagree about the appraisal, there should be an appeal or review procedure. Normally the manager's boss and/or HR manager will review the appraisal.

Implementation

After the appraisal, job descriptions may need amending. Sometimes standards/targets are set or revised later. It is *essential* that both parties have clear, specific action plans to implement and support agreed changes. Otherwise, it has been a waste of time!

Regular, structured reviews

Managers need to keep 'a finger on the pulse' by monitoring commitments and progress by both parties, *never less than quarterly*.

Conducting motivational appraisals tests the manager's effectiveness in managing and developing their staff.

These guidelines, and their implementation through personal action and development plans and regular reviews, are the basis for implementing successful performance management and meeting your objectives.

Summary checklist

✓ Prepare thoroughly for appraisal – the investment you make in the future performance and success of your staff and yourself.

✓ Review and update job descriptions.

✓ Hold pre-meetings to brief those being appraised and help them prepare.

✓ The appraisee's attitude is the manager's responsibility.

✓ Open up discussion by following the agenda dependency sequence.

✓ Ask 'open' questions, gain self-appraisal, examples and valid evidence.

✓ Encourage the sharing of specific, reinforcing, developmental feedback.

✓ Ensure implementation through action and development plans and regular reviews.

Bibliography

Competency, The Journal of Performance Through People, IRS

Forrest, Andrew, *5-Way Management*, The Industrial Society, 1997

France, Steve, *360° Appraisal*, The Industrial Society, 1997

IDS Studies, Personnel Policy Practice – Appraisal Systems, Incomes Data Services Limited, April 1999

Lawson, Ian, *Appraisal and Appraisal Interviewing*, The Industrial Society Press 1987, third edition 1989

Managing Best Practice No 37 – Appraisal, The Industrial Society

Managing Best Practice No 71 – Performance Measurement, The Industrial Society

Moores, Roger, *Managing for High Performance*, The Industrial Society Press, 1994

Glossary of terms

Aims or goals
Aims or goals are something to be aimed at in general.

Competencies
Competencies identify the skill, task or performance factor to be carried out. They define and describe in a specific, measurable way the competence level to which it is to be carried out.

Dependency sequence
The dependency sequence identifies the order in which things have to be done (sequentially), when one is dependent on another being carried out first.

Developmental feedback
Developmental feedback aims, through the use of specific questions and examples, to enable individuals to self-assess, and to develop insight into cause and effect. It is aimed at helping individuals learn from their behaviour and results, and to develop their own solutions.

Feedback
Feedback is communication that reflects back to the individual information about what they say and do – their behaviour and its effect on others. It is observable, and provides specific examples. It involves sharing ideas, offering suggestions, advice and solutions.

Job descriptions

Job descriptions provide a clear, relevant understanding of what the job consists of, inputs and outcomes expected, including:

- The nature of the job.
- Accountability, key responsibilities and relationships.
- The objectives, why the job exists.
- Key result areas, tasks and responsibilities.
- The standards of performance, competencies and outcomes.
- Working conditions and training and development.

Key result areas

Key result areas are key tasks and responsibilities which enable people to focus on and meet the objectives of their job, in terms of deadlines, customer service, quality, output and profitability, etc.

Mission

The mission outlines the purpose for which the organisation exists. It sets out:

- What the company is in business to achieve.
- How it will do this.
- Where it sees itself in the future.

Objectives

Key overall goals, objectives of the business. An individual objective is an object of thought, feeling or action. The object of our efforts that achieves:

- The mission, business plan.
- The required result.

One-to-one reviews

A one-to-one review is a regular meeting between an individual and their manager to review performance progress. One-to-ones are planned, prepared and recorded following a structured outline, with actions and outcomes.

Performance appraisal

The individual's performance, outcomes, behaviour, skills and competencies are the focus for the appraisal, *not* their personal characteristics.

Performance standards

Performance standards are a measure *for the job*. They provide a defined, specific measure of what is adequate for some job or purpose.

Service-level agreements

An agreement between the supplier and internal or external customer, defining in a specific measurable way the level or standard of service between the two parties.

Specific

Specific means expressed in exact, identified terms, denoted by the use of numbers or nouns (proper or common).

Targets

Targets are set for *individuals*, based on their current performance. They are specific, measurable, timed future actions, to motivate and challenge. They gauge progress in achieving objectives, standards, competencies and tasks, and encourage self-assessment.

360° appraisal

With 360° appraisal the manager is appraised holistically through feedback from all their main contacts, eg their direct reports, manager, colleagues, peers, customers, suppliers.

Traditional appraisal

With traditional appraisal the manager appraises and reviews their staff's performance, which may involve rating them.

Upwards or 180° appraisal

With upwards or 180° appraisal the direct reports review their manager's performance, skills and processes through upwards feedback.

Values

Values are the beliefs the oganisation holds, which guide daily decisions and actions.

Vision

The vision is a realistic long-term ambition, which gives the company a clear sense of direction.